KEVIN SINF13LD

MY LEAGUE YEARS
IN WORDS AND PICTURES

WRITTEN WITH

PETER SMITH

PICTURE EDITOR: STEVE RIDING

GREAT NORTHERN

Great Northern Books Limited
PO Box 213, Ilkley, LS29 9WS
www.greatnorthernbooks.co.uk

ISBN: 978-0-9933447-2-5

Picture Editor: Steve Riding

Images © Yorkshire Evening Post, unless stated.

Design: David Burrill

CIP Data
A catalogue for this book is available from the
British Library

Supported by

LEEDS
BECKETT
UNIVERSITY

ACKNOWLEDGEMENTS

Kevin Sinfield: "I'd like to thank all the players and coaches I have worked with throughout my time in rugby league and all the staff at Headingley, as well as the fans who have given me such fantastic support.

"Thanks to Peter Smith, Steve Riding, Barry Cox, Leeds Beckett University and Jonny Wilkinson for their help and support with this book.

"To my parents, Ray and Beryl, thanks for your love and support and the sacrifices which made everything possible. Also to my sister Stephanie and brother Ian, for always being there for me.

"To my wife Jayne and my two boys Jack and Sam, thanks for your constant love and the happiness you have given me. Through the good times and bad, you have always been my rocks."

Peter Smith would like to thank Steve Riding for his excellent work as picture editor, as well as all the other photographers whose images are included in these pages.

Also: Barry, David, Pat and everyone at Great Northern Books; everyone at Yorkshire Post Newspapers, particularly Ian Day and Nicola Furbisher; Stuart Martel and Daniel Spencer for their expertise and Janet Harrison and Luke Smith for constant support.

Photography

Images in chapter one courtesy of the Sinfield Family.

Yorkshire Evening Post: Steve Riding, Jonathan Gawthorpe, Bruce Rollinson, Tony Johnson, Mark Bickerdike, Simon Hulme, James Hardisty, Gerard Binks, Gary Longbottom, Dan Oxtoby, Justin Lloyd, Mike Cowling.

Dave Williams *RLPhotos.com*

PA/Press Association Images, Reuters, Sky Sports.

CONTENTS

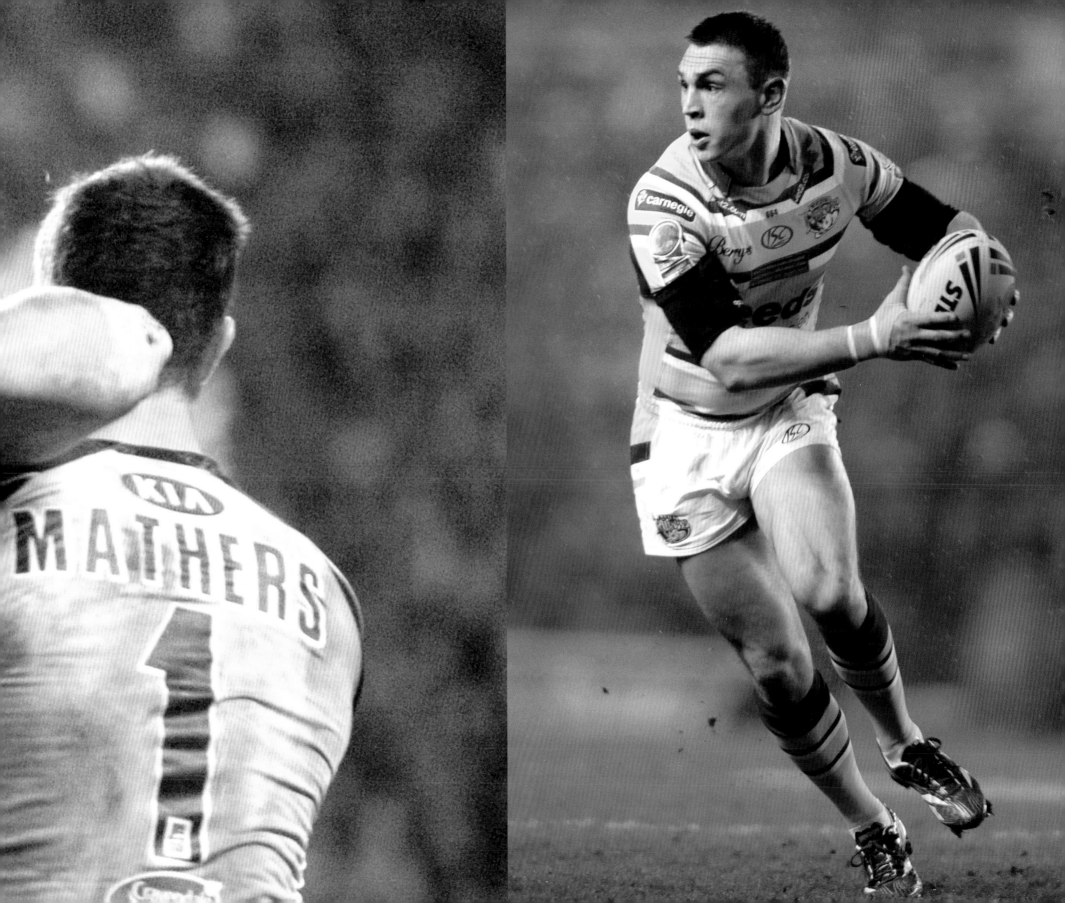

FOREWORD

BY JONNY WILKINSON CBE

ENGLAND AND BRITISH LIONS RUGBY UNION LEGEND

Kevin Sinfield is a huge name in British rugby and I was delighted when I heard a book was being produced to celebrate his achievements with Leeds Rhinos.

As a big fan of rugby league I have followed Kev's career closely and we have met on a few occasions, getting to know each other personally in recent years. The first thing to say is he is every bit as decent and professional off the field as he appears on it.

There is no doubt Kev is a fantastic player and it is exceptionally difficult to comprehend him being at the top of his game for so many years. He will certainly be remembered as one of the modern greats, but it rankles with me when people try to compare one player to another.

Arguments over who was or is the better player are impossible in rugby, which is all about the team. In either code, your mentality is to do your best for your team. Every player tries to exhibit the leadership necessary to influence the performance of those around him and that is why Kev is such a great example.

Even looking on from the outside, it is obvious Kev is a team player. For 19 seasons, game after game, he has inspired his

team towards more and on an individual level he has never stopped trying to improve.

To do that on a consistent basis and perform with the level of excellence he has over such a long period is the mark of greatness. We will never know what would have happened if he had played for other teams. It certainly would have been interesting to see him compete in Australia, but his loyalty to Leeds is unquestioned and what he has done for the Rhinos is impeccable.

It is fair to say Kev is a role model. This is because he goes about his business with the utmost integrity - not only in rugby, but also in life. For me, it is this honesty which has driven the quality of what we have all seen from him on the field.

When Kev goes out to play rugby he is not trying to do anything different or be something he is not; it is business as usual.

For his rugby league career to end the way it did was the perfect scenario and he thoroughly deserves the plaudits and recognition which have come his way since.

I wish him well with this book and everything he does in the future.

8

INTRODUCTION

After 19 seasons and 521 games, Kevin Sinfield is no longer British sport's best kept secret.

Sinfield's final act as a Leeds Rhinos player was to lift the Super League trophy for a seventh time, but that was not the end of the story.

For so long ignored by the national media Sinfield, a hero in his adopted city, finally achieved wider acclaim in December, 2015 – two months after his Grand Final glory – when he was selected among 12 nominees for the BBC's iconic Sports Personality of the Year award.

He was the first rugby league player to be shortlisted in the honour's 61-year history and his inclusion began one of the most remarkable periods of his glittering career. Rugby league is a fiercely tribal sport, but there are occasions when its northern heartland unites to show the rest of the country what it is missing.

This was one of those times as more than a quarter of a million votes were cast for Sinfield, who finished a hugely creditable runner-up to tennis ace Andy Murray. For once, rugby league was in the spotlight and the sport could not have wished for a better ambassador.

By then, ironically, the 35-year-old Sinfield was plying his trade in rugby union with Yorkshire Carnegie, but he remains a rugby league man at heart. Born in Oldham, he first picked

up an oval ball aged seven and always seemed destined for the very top.

Rated as the finest schoolboy player of his generation, he was courted by a host of leading clubs before opting to join Leeds just as rugby league was entering a new era of full-time professionalism and preparing to switch to a summer season.

Appointed captain of Leeds at the end of 2002, he was to carry the armband for the next 13 years, leading the club through the greatest period in its history and becoming the finest skipper rugby league – and arguably British sport – has ever seen.

The statistics give an indication of what Sinfield achieved during his 19 seasons in Leeds Rhinos' first team. Nobody has played more games or scored more points in Super League; Sinfield holds the record for most Grand Final wins as captain and is the third-highest points scorer in the code's history, which dates back to 1895.

As well as seven Grand Final victories, he steered Rhinos to the Super League leaders' shield and World Club title three times and the Challenge Cup twice - and on top of all that he has managed to remain one of the most humble and grounded individuals in sport.

Sinfield's most glorious season at Leeds was his last. He

captained Rhinos to a record-breaking 50-0 win over Hull KR at Wembley and played a crucial role as they climbed off the floor to claim top spot on the Super League table, with a sensational last-gasp win away to Huddersfield Giants.

And so on to Old Trafford and a showdown with Wigan Warriors. Leeds led at half-time, but found themselves four points behind going into the final quarter. Josh Walters' try levelled the scores and Sinfield kicked a conversion which proved the difference between the sides at the final whistle. His 1,792nd goal and 3,967th point for Leeds completed the treble and the club's greatest year.

It was the perfect ending, but Sinfield's rugby league career was not all wine and roses. He was dropped for the 2000 Challenge Cup final and blamed when Leeds were beaten in the decider three years later. It took 17 years of trying and five losers' medals before he finally got his hands on rugby league's most famous knockout trophy.

Even in his all-conquering final campaign Sinfield had to overcome the sort of adversity which might have crushed other players. After a spell on the injured list, he was dropped to the bench and then from the team altogether before returning to inspire the clean sweep.

Whenever he was down, Sinfield got up again. The classic example was at Old Trafford in 2012, against Warrington Wolves, when Leeds' captain was knocked out early in the second half, but rallied to win his second Harry Sunderland award as Grand Final man of the match.

No one player makes a team and Sinfield's reign as captain came at a time when the club fielded a side packed with exceptional local talent, supplemented by some key signings from home and abroad. But Sinfield was the beating heart of Rhinos throughout his two decades at the club and it is hard to believe Headingley's trophy cabinet would have been so full had he opted to join Warrington or Wigan when he had the chance in the early 1990s.

A model professional on and off the field, Sinfield was awarded an MBE in 2014 and is known in Leeds as 'Sir Kev'. This is the history of his rugby league career from his earliest days at Oldham amateur club Waterhead to the treble-clinching victory over Wigan.

In the following pages he reveals the background to his greatest moments and how he found the motivation to bounce back from the deepest of lows. It is also a tribute to the players he has played alongside and against, the coaches who have shaped his career and fans who have supported him throughout.

CHAPTER ONE
FROM WATERHEAD TO HEADINGLEY
1988-1999

The first time he walked through the main gates at Headingley Stadium, Kevin Sinfield felt at home.

Leeds weren't the obvious choice of professional club for an Oldham lad and proud Lancastrian and if it had not been for chief scout Bob Pickles' quick thinking – and sharp ears - Sinfield might have ended up at one of the powerhouses on the western side of the Pennines.

Born in Oldham on September 12, 1980, Sinfield was seven years old when he first picked up a rugby ball, at local amateur side Waterhead. His older brother, Ian, was already a junior there and Sinfield recalled: "He came home one day and told my mum and dad the under-nines were short of players and was I interested?

"I went a couple of weeks later, on a Saturday morning. Ian had gone off to train with the under-11s and left me with the nines. I didn't know anybody and I remember shedding a tear, standing there on my own. But very quickly I got pulled into the group and suddenly I had 20 new mates. We started hitting tackle bags and getting muddy and it was a really good start. From that moment, I fell in love with the game.

"I have got great memories of Waterhead and I made some lifelong friends. I think that's where you get a lot of your values, from those early times. Two of my best mates are from there and those days were very kind."

Having introduced Sinfield to rugby league, elder brother Ian was a big influence on Kevin, not only in his junior days, but also throughout his career. "Growing up, I shared a room with Ian until our sister Steph went to university. When she moved out I lost a sister and gained a bedroom!

"Ian and I are close and I learned a lot off him. He was a good player and should have played at the top level. I have told him if he had been at Leeds he would have played in Super League 10 years ago. We are very different, but he was fit and he would have made a good modern-day front-rower. In the Leeds team of the mid-2000s, when we needed bigger men who could last big minutes, he would have been ideal. It's a shame he never got an opportunity."

The young Sinfield played for Waterhead through to under-15 level and quickly established himself as a natural talent. He represented Lancashire at every age group from under-nines and was made captain of the 10s, an honour he held on to for the rest of his time in the junior ranks.

"We had a decent side at Waterhead," he said. "In the under-12 season we went unbeaten and we won the Lancashire Cup at under-12s, 13s and 14s, which is pretty uncommon for a team from Oldham. With Lancashire I can only remember being beaten by Yorkshire once, when Jamie Jones-Buchanan was playing for them.

"I played against him all the way through and my first game

with him was for England Schoolboys, which was my last match as an amateur. That was the start of a great friendship."

Throughout his junior days Sinfield played as a goal-kicking loose-forward. He took duties with the boot from the day he won a kicking contest after training at Waterhead, as a 10-year-old.

"My mate's dad, Mick Hough, was our coach," Sinfield recalled. "He sadly passed away a few years ago, but he was a big influence on me as a junior. I remember having a kicking competition after training one day; I did all right and got the job. It was mine from then on. I loved kicking anyway and I spent lots of time as a kid practising goal kicking with my mates. I also used to go a couple of times a week with my dad Ray. We took a bucket of sand to use as a tee and just kicked goals. It's something I have always done and loved doing."

Early highlights included an appearance at Wembley in the under-11 schoolboys' curtain-raiser to the 1992 Challenge Cup final. Sinfield captained Oldham Schools against Batley/Dewsbury and scored a try and three goals in a 22-6 victory.

From the age of 11 Sinfield and several of his teammates began to attract the attention of scouts from top Lancashire clubs, particularly Wigan and Warrington. He went on trial at both and did part of a pre-season at Wigan as a 12-year-old, when future Leeds teammate Barrie McDermott was in the first team squad, alongside legends of the game including Shaun Edwards and Martin Offiah.

He said: "I came very close to signing for both Wigan and Warrington. I played for Lancashire against Yorkshire at Wakefield and Bob Pickles was there. The following day we got a phone call and he invited me and my parents over for talks with Doug Laughton, who was Leeds' coach at the time.

"Wigan's scout was at the game and he made a comment

LANCASHIRE PRIDE...Kevin Sinfield played early representative rugby for Lancashire. They went through the age groups unbeaten.

BEST MATE...Kevin Sinfield and his Oldham best mate Gaz Barber played together for North West Counties and Lancashire.

STARTING OUT...Kevin Sinfield was tipped as a potential star from his early days in rugby league, with Lancashire and his school team St Agnes.

YOUNG HOPEFULS...Lancashire under-11s and under-13s were a breeding ground for the professional game.

FAMOUS FACES: After Oldham Schools played at Wembley in 1992 a starstruck Kevin Sinfield rubbed shoulders with players from the Challenge Cup final, including Castleford Tigers' Tawera Nikau, Lee Crooks and Mike Ford.

about them maybe signing me and I think Bob heard that and got straight on to Doug Laughton. Along with my dad we had a meeting with Doug and the place just felt right. Walking through the old gates at Headingley, it had a great feel to it and it meant I was out of all the politics in Lancashire."

Sinfield added: "At the time, some young lads were getting a chance at Leeds, the likes of Matt Schultz, Paul Cook and Franny Cummins and that is all I ever wanted, a chance. Warrington offered almost double the money Leeds did, Wigan were very similar to Leeds, but Leeds just felt right.

"We had the meeting with Doug and he came back with an offer, which we accepted. His actual words were 'If I can get you this amount, will you sign today'? As a 13-year-old kid I replied 'no, my mum's not here'! But it was all agreed, Doug came to our house the following day and I signed."

Ellery Hanley's presence at Leeds was another factor behind Sinfield's decision to move to Headingley, rather than Wigan or Warrington. The former Great Britain captain and coach was the young Sinfield's rugby league hero and he said: "He was everything I wanted to be. People often feel let down when they meet their heroes, but Ellery was every bit as good as I expected him to be. He had so much time for me and he was an absolute gentleman."

The club Sinfield signed for, on August 1, 1994, was very different to the Leeds he left 21 years later. Wigan were the dominant force in the game, with Leeds spending big money in an attempt to close the gap. They had not won a trophy since 1988 and were heading for a financial crisis which was to lead to a takeover by chairman Paul Caddick and chief executive Gary Hetherington at the end of the 1996 season, the first of rugby league's summer era.

WEMBLEY-BOUND...A top kicker from his early days, Kevin Sinfield's biggest day as a junior was at Wembley in 1992 with Oldham Schools.

Top and left: MAGIC BOOT...A young Kevin Sinfield shows off the kicking style which was to become so familiar to Leeds Rhinos fans.

HALLOWED TURF...Oldham Schools' captain Kevin Sinfield kicked three goals in their Wembley win over Dewsbury and Batley.

In Sinfield's early days at Leeds the club ran an under-19s academy side and a reserve 'A' team. Carrying the tag of 'England's best schoolboy player', Sinfield was soon turning out in both lower grade outfits.

He made his debut for the academy alongside George Rayner, Gary Smith and Jamie Jones-Buchanan and played most of the 1997 and 1998 seasons at that level. Of his 'A' team debut, he remembered: "It was about six weeks into the season. The 'A' team played on Wednesday nights and Leeds were playing Salford at Headingley.

"My brother Ian was playing for Salford, so I came over to watch with my mum, Beryl, and dad. Somebody dropped out in the warm-up, so I got pulled in and given a pair of boots and I played the last 15 minutes off the bench. It was the only time I ever played against Ian."

By early 1997, Sinfield was one of three Oldham-based players at Leeds, alongside McDermott and Iestyn Harris. They travelled together to training, meaning Sinfield had an early insight into two of that generation's top stars.

McDermott is somebody else Sinfield credits as being a key influence. The hardman prop also came from the Waterhead club, via Oldham and Wigan and Sinfield described him as being like another older brother. He said: "Baz was absolutely brilliant with me.

"He made some mistakes in his time, but he was always willing to give me good advice and support. He was a rock for me and still is today. We played together and travelled together and I know even now if I need anything, he will be there for me."

Having McDermott watching his back was a bonus for Sinfield when he eventually broke into the first team. "I knew at any stage if somebody tried to step over the line, Baz would sort it," Sinfield remembered.

"To have the backing of someone who was so influential - and feared at times - was brilliant and made my career at the

Top: PASS MASTER...Playing for Lancashire under-13s, Kevin Sinfield gets set to send his winger on a run.

Bottom: ON TRIAL...Kevin Sinfield had a trial for England Schools under-16s, during his under-15s season. The player in blue at Keighley's Cougar Park is future Leeds teammate Andy Speak.

start so much easier."

When Hetherington and Caddick took over the club in 1996, more emphasis was placed on attracting local players and bringing young talent through into the first team. Leeds were developing an outstanding academy side and dominated at that level for a decade.

Sinfield was part of the team which won the academy championship in 1997, 1998 – beating Wigan in the Grand Final – and 1999, when Warrington were defeated in a title-decider at St Helens' Knowsley Road.

Top academy games were televised by Sky Sports at the time, so Sinfield was beginning to attract attention as an outstanding prospect, not only at Leeds, but also among the wider rugby league public.

"The 1998 academy team was a brilliant side," Sinfield recalled. "We won the Grand Final, which was at Headingley before Rhinos played St Helens in the Super League play-off semi-final. We did a walk-around at Old Trafford during half-time in the Super League Grand Final, between Leeds and Wigan."

Sinfield rates the 1998 academy Grand Final success as highly as any of his later achievements, but has less fond memories of the following

LOCAL HERO...Before a game for Waterhead under-14s.

THE FIRST TEST...Kevin Sinfield made his England Schools under-16s debut when he was still qualified for under-15 rugby.

year, when he was drafted in as a 'ringer'.

"I was qualified to play," he said. "But I was embarrassed about it. I had played 21 first team games that year and I felt horrible about it because I had taken somebody else's spot. You have to do as you're told and I ended up playing."

Dean Bell was the coach who gave

Sinfield his first team debut, in 1997. At the end of that campaign the former New Zealand international moved into a new role as youth boss, so was heavily involved in Sinfield's early years at the club.

Sinfield said: "When I first went to Leeds he spent a lot of time with me. He didn't really know me, but I think he liked my enthusiasm, coming over from Oldham.

NAME: _K SINFIELD_____ D.o.B. _12-9-80__

AGE: _13___ AVERAGE AGE of GROUP _12·9_M PLAYING POSITION _LF____ HT. _5'8"_ WT. _9st 10lbs._

PHYSICAL TESTS	RESULT	AVERAGE	POSITION IN GROUP	SKILLS TESTS	RESULT	AVERAGE	POSITION IN GROUP
VO2 MAX.	11.1	10.3	4				
SPEED(15m)	2.79	2.9	2				
SPEED(40m)	5.9	6.00	6				
SGT. JUMP	17"	13"	1	Already completed Silver award			
SIT-UPS	67	55	7				
PRESS-UPS	40	38	5				
STRENGTH	-	-					

PHYSICAL CONDITION:-

COMMENTS _Kevin came very high in the physical tests and must ensure that he continues to keep himself in peak condition._

SKILLS:-

FINAL AWARD: _____

COMMENTS _Very high skill level has all the attributes of a highly skilled performer._

TACTICAL UNDERSTANDING:- _Excellent understanding of the tactical plays of RL Communicates well listens and asks question a good leader._

ATTITUDE & COMMITMENT:- _First class attitude wants to be a winner very helpful full of determination._

ADVICE:- _Needs to keep practising the skills of RL. to always listen to his coaches Kevin could develop into a quality player._

COACHES: _D I Wyl_

BRITISH RUGBY LEAGUE COACHING SCHEME
LANCASTER UNIVERSITY   JULY 1993.....

Dean was all about working hard and making sacrifices and dedication and commitment and I like to think he saw in me some of the traits he had as a player.

"He was a lovely man. He gave me a book, called The Edge, which I have still got. It is an old book, full of inspirational quotes. Somebody had given it to him early in his career and he passed it on to me. Dean has an aura about him and he was great for the young kids who played under him.

"We had a very good academy team and Dean ran it like a professional side. We trained on an evening, but we trained like a Super League outfit. It was a good time. Look back at that team, there were people like Danny Ward, Jamie Jones, Garreth Carvell...It was some side. A lot of us went on to play first team, either at Leeds or somewhere else.

"We were very, very hard to beat and a really good team to play in. I honestly think, if we'd had the chance, we would have beaten a lot of Division One teams. It was important because it was the start of young lads getting a chance at Leeds."

ON REPORT... The British Rugby League Coaching Scheme's assessment of Kevin at the age of 13 reveals he was already showing massive promise.

SUITS YOU...Kevin Sinfield made an impression for England under-16s in 1996.

BOWING OUT...Oldham Schools, including Kevin Sinfield, won the England Schools Cup in 1996. His final game as an amateur was for England Schools the following year.

Left: A NEW START...Kevin Sinfield and his fellow intake prepare for their Leeds Rhinos academy debut.
(Dave Williams)

Top right: ELDER BROTHER...Ian Sinfield, seen here playing for Swinton in 2004, was and remains one of Kevin's greatest influences.
(Dave Williams)

Bottom right: CHIMING IN... Dean Bell was the coach who gave Kevin Sinfield his Leeds Rhinos debut. The Kiwi, seen here scoring in a one-off playing appearance against Paris in 1996, replaced Doug Laughton, who had signed the teenage starlet.

CHAPTER TWO
BREAKING THROUGH

1997-2001

Leeds Rhinos' 24-22 defeat to Sheffield Eagles at Headingley on August 22, 1997, was memorable for one reason only. The 9,813 fans present that day witnessed the start of one of the club's - and rugby league's - greatest careers.

Kevin Sinfield made his debut that day and he remembered: "After about four or five games in the 'A' team I got a phone call from Dean Bell, who was the first team coach. I was 16 and it was the day before I got my GCSE results.

"He said 'Can you come in for training tomorrow? You are playing on Friday'. That was on the Wednesday. My mum and dad picked my GCSE results up on the Thursday and I travelled over to Leeds with Barrie and Iestyn for training and I played on the Friday night."

Sinfield came off the bench for Leeds, who were second in the Super League table. The home side led 22-14 with three minutes remaining, but two late tries and a touchline conversion by Mark Aston earned Sheffield a shock win.

It was a disappointing start, but for Sinfield making his debut so early in his career provided a valuable lesson. He said: "I came to Leeds for an opportunity and I couldn't have had a better one. It was an important moment in my career, not just because it was my debut, but because it made me realise that physically and mentally I wasn't ready to play at that level.

"I had only been playing against men for a few weeks in the 'A' team and I realised then I had a lot of work to do to play at that level every week and to compete every week. It was a really proud moment, but a big learning experience."

Sinfield's second game came just three days later, on a Bank Holiday Monday and also ended in a loss, this time 25-18 at St Helens. Garreth Carvell, another player who was to have a long and successful Super League career, though not for Leeds, also made his Rhinos debut, but it was a mixed afternoon for Sinfield. He came off the bench and made a break to set up a try for winger Leroy Rivett, his first significant contribution in the senior team, but suffered an ankle injury moments later which put him out of action for the rest of the year.

By 1998 Sinfield had been offered a full-time contract, but he decided to stay at Oldham Sixth Form College to complete his 'A' Levels. At that stage he was training in Oldham before studies and during his lunch hour and then driving to Leeds, having passed his test four weeks after his 17th birthday, to train with the academy.

The 1998 season saw Sinfield make two more appearances, against Salford in a game played at Gateshead and away to Huddersfield Giants. Leeds beat Salford 34-16 for Sinfield's first Super League win and Huddersfield were crushed 72-16, when he scored his maiden touchdown. He recalled: "I got the ball off Iestyn and went through a hole about 20 metres out, with the full-back out of position."

Sinfield's first goal for Rhinos didn't come until June, 1999, when he converted twice in a 50-22 Headingley win over Castleford Tigers. By that stage the teenage prospect was beginning to establish himself in Leeds' senior side. He played 21 times in the 1999 season, nine of them in the starting line-up. It was a successful year for Rhinos who followed up on the previous season's Grand Final appearance by winning the Challenge Cup, thrashing London Broncos 52-16 at Wembley.

Sinfield didn't feature that afternoon, but was a substitute in the team which beat hosts Widnes Vikings 46-10 at the quarter-final stage. Widnes, then a lower division side, came out firing and gave Rhinos a fright in the first half, which ended 10-10.

Leeds needed something special to break the underdogs' resistance and Sinfield provided it with a quick-fire brace of touchdowns, the first coming just four minutes after he had replaced the injured Marc Glanville.

"It was a good year," Sinfield said of the 1999 campaign. "Graham Murray was coach and he did some wonderful things. I was in and around some fantastic players and it was a great experience to be part of the Challenge Cup final squad, even though I didn't play.

"I did get a medal, but I probably didn't realise its worth until I'd lost five Challenge Cup finals. For me to devalue it and say it was worthless would go against everything we had put together, that you win and lose together as a squad, not just as a team. How could I talk to young kids who haven't played and tell them their medal means something, if I didn't value mine? After I had lost five finals people would say to me 'it's a real shame you haven't got a Cup medal' and I could tell them 'actually, I have'.

Rhinos were a team on the up in both 1998 and 1999. The

KICK UP THE BACKSIDE...Graham Murray, who coached Rhinos in 1998 and 1999, was a hard task master. Sinfield received a "rollicking" from the coach following this game at Sheffield Eagles.

first Super League season, 1996, was a disaster for Leeds as the cash-strapped club finished third from bottom in the table, above only Paris and Workington Town and below teams including Sheffield, Halifax and Oldham.

The takeover at the end of that campaign brought a fresh approach, plus an injection of cash. With Dean Bell still in charge Leeds were more competitive in 1997, though they faded late in the year to finish fifth in the table.

At the end of 1997 Bell stepped down as coach to take over his new role in charge of the club's youth setup and Murray

A LEARNING PROCESS...Rhinos' youngsters, captained by Kevin Sinfield, swept all before them on their way to winning the Academy Grand Final.

NUMBER'S UP...In the autumn of 1999 Sinfield was awarded the iconic number he was to wear for the next 16 seasons. Chev Walker also received a squad number that year.

was brought in from Australia as team boss. Having previously guided Hunter Mariners to the World Club Championship final, Murray transformed Rhinos' fortunes, on the back of some key signings. Harris had arrived from Warrington the previous season and Glanville, Brad Godden and Daryl Powell all made their debut in 1998 and were to prove hugely influential.

Murray returned to Australia at the end of 1999 and had spells coaching Sydney Roosters and North Queensland Cowboys in the National Rugby League (NRL), as well as New South Wales at State of Origin level. Tragically, he died following a heart attack in 2013, aged only 58.

Sinfield said: "Graham was a big disciplinarian, very strict, but a fantastic coach. He had a way about him that made you want to play for him. He was very big on team spirit and I learned a lot under Graham; I remember Paul Sterling and myself getting strips torn off us after a game in Sheffield one day. Things like that help to mould you and I think it's a shame he didn't stay longer than he did. He had a huge influence on the club and I think if he had stayed the success that came later on might have arrived sooner."

Another Australian, Dean Lance, was appointed coach for the 2000 season. Ahead of that campaign Sinfield was allocated squad number 13, which he was to keep for the rest of his Leeds career. When Sinfield first wore the No 13 jersey, the next player to inherit it, Stevie Ward, was just six years old.

The 2000 season began poorly for Leeds who lost their first five Super League games, while also reaching a second successive Challenge Cup final. The showpiece, which was moved to Murrayfield in Edinburgh during work to rebuild Wembley, was almost postponed when a near-by river burst its banks.

A huge clean-up effort enabled the final to go ahead as planned, but Sinfield once again had to watch from the sidelines. That had been expected a year earlier, but the Cup decider was the first game he missed in 2000, Lance opting to select prop Jamie Mathiou among his substitutes instead.

"That was my first big disappointment," Sinfield admitted. "Looking back, it was horrendous, just a horrible moment in my career. I had played every game up to then, I was man of the match in the semi-final and when we beat Huddersfield in the home game the week before.

"I wasn't banking on it, but I thought I was very close to playing. To realise on the Wednesday before the game I wouldn't be playing was completely heart breaking. All my family and friends were going to the final and I knew how much

SMART COOKIE...Passing his 'A' levels allowed Kevin Sinfield to focus entirely on rugby league for the first time.

COACH DRIVER...Graham Murray steered Kevin Sinfield in the right direction during his early days in Rhinos' full-time squad.

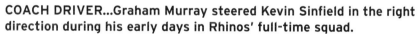

HOMECOMING...Coach Graham Murray and captain Iestyn Harris show off the Challenge Cup at Headingley after Rhinos' 1999 Cup final success. Kevin Sinfield played in the quarter-final, but wasn't a member of the Wembley team.

AXED...Dean Lance coached Leeds in 2000, but was sacked early the following season. He dropped Kevin Sinfield from Rhinos' team for the 2000 Challenge Cup final.

NEW BROOM...Daryl Powell took over as Leeds coach in 2001 and set about improving the club's culture. His greatest legacy was appointing Kevin Sinfield as captain.

A NEW HOPE...The emergence of young prospects Rob Burrow, Mark Calderwood and Matt Diskin was one of the positives from Rhinos' disappointing 2001 campaign.

it meant to my mum and dad. To have to go home and tell them I hadn't made the team was really, really tough.

"On the day itself I remember filling up with tears when the teams came out at the start of the game. It was a horrible experience, but looking back now it was another big moment for me. It made me evaluate where I was and what I wanted to get out of the game. It was my first real challenge, to get myself up off the canvas and come back fighting. You get a lot of respect from the rest of the team if you conduct yourself properly and I tried to do that."

Leeds were beaten 24-18 by Bradford Bulls in a final which was closer than many pundits had expected. They then bounced back to win 15 of their next 17 games, including 13 successive victories. After their dreadful start fourth place

on the table was a respectable finish, but Bradford ended their season by eliminating them in the second round of the play-offs, at Odsal.

Lance remained in charge the following season, which began with a club-record 106-10 thrashing of Swinton in the Challenge Cup fourth round. Sinfield contributed two tries to the historic total and missed just one game that year. He crossed 10 times and kicked 29 goals and a drop in 33 matches, all but one of those appearances being in the starting line-up.

It was a season of change for Rhinos. Lance was axed in April and Powell, who had retired at the end of the previous campaign to take over as youth boss, stepped in as coach. Just as significant was Harris' exit late in the year, when he

made a big-money move to play rugby union in Wales.

Leeds were hit hard by injuries throughout 2001, but that gave Powell an opportunity to blood some promising youngsters, including Matt Diskin, Rob Burrow, Mark Calderwood and Danny McGuire. Rhinos finished fifth, suffered a 62-18 drubbing by Bradford Bulls in their final league match, at Valley Parade and fell at the first hurdle in the play-offs, away to St Helens.

Sinfield, Francis Cummins and Rob Burrow, who had made his debut early in the season, shared kicking duties following Harris' departure, but Leeds' management opted to bring in another goal-kicking stand-off, Australian Ben Walker, for the 2002 season.

He had been top points scorer in the NRL before he joined Leeds and landed 119 goals that year, but never made the impact Rhinos' coaching staff had hoped for. Powell experimented by switching him to full-back for a spell and he also spent time out of the side before leaving at the end of the year.

Burrow and Sinfield were back-up goal kickers – under new captain Cummins - and Kevin also filled in for Walker at stand-off. He finished the year with eight tries and 32 goals from 30 starts and two appearances as a substitute. For Leeds it was another disappointing campaign as they finished fourth in the table and lost at St Helens in the second round of the play-offs. Saints also beat them in the semi-finals of the Challenge Cup, for the second successive season.

It wasn't all doom and gloom though. Rhinos avenged the previous season's humiliation with a brilliant 17-4 triumph at Bradford in the opening round of the Challenge Cup and ended their league campaign with a memorable 33-26 victory at Wigan Warriors.

CHAPTER THREE
A CAPTAIN'S SLOG
2002-2003

At the end of 2002 it was obvious changes would have to be made if Leeds were to shake off their tag as rugby league's great under-achievers.

In seven seasons of summer rugby they had won the Challenge Cup, been runners-up and reached the inaugural Grand Final, but still lagged behind the big-three of Bradford Bulls, St Helens and Wigan Warriors.

It was not good enough and coach Daryl Powell reacted to the disappointment of the previous season by axing Ryan Sheridan, Andy Hay and Karl Pratt – all first team regulars and Great Britain internationals - from his squad. That was a shock to fans, teammates and the players themselves, but one decision made in the winter of 2002 was to have a lasting impact: He asked Kevin Sinfield if he would take over as captain.

"Franny Cummins had been captain the previous year," Sinfield said. "Daryl was making some changes and I think he just wanted a fresh start. I remember him talking to me and saying he thought I could make a good captain and did I fancy doing the job next year?

"I can remember being elated, so happy, but straight away thinking of Franny. He had been fantastic with me; he had been in a similar situation, coming through into the first team as a young kid and he'd been a big help to me from the moment I signed in 1994. I knew what being captain meant to

him so before I accepted I asked Daryl if I could speak to Franny.

"I rang Franny and he was absolutely brilliant, he said he would back me no matter what. He was genuinely so delighted for me and that's what he is like, a top bloke. He always had the team and the club at heart and he always put the team first. That's quite a tough thing to do at times, but Franny was always very unselfish in the way he approached the game. He had so much time for the younger lads and it was great to have his support and backing and from the likes of Barrie McDermott, who was brilliant as well."

Sinfield was 22 when he took over the captaincy in December, 2002. At that stage nobody could have predicted he would hold the honour for the next 13 seasons, but the man himself was confident he would do the role justice, despite his young age.

"I felt ready for it and I had learned a lot off Iestyn and people like Barrie Mac," he said. "Commuting with Barrie and Iestyn we had some interesting journeys from Oldham to Leeds. They were both Great Britain internationals with good habits and values and they were happy times when we travelled together.

"Iestyn was a great captain for Leeds. Some of his performances during the couple of years I played alongside him were unbelievable and I think people forget just how

ROLE MODEL...Wigan and Great Britain captain Andy Farrell was one of the players Kevin Sinfield aspired to emulate.

FEARSOME SIGHT...Barrie McDermott was one of Super League's most notorious hardmen, a reputation which kept the young Kevin Sinfield safe up against more experienced opponents.

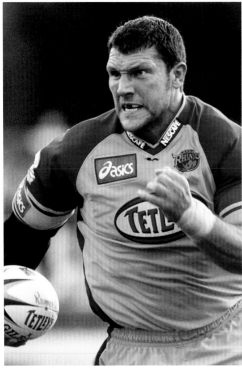

good he was. He was Man of Steel in 1998 and the best player in the competition by a mile at that time."

Taking the captaincy was also an opportunity for Sinfield to emulate one of his role models in the wider game, Wigan's Andy Farrell. "He's somebody I looked up to. He played for Wigan at a young age and played loose-forward and stand-off. Physically we were very different, but he is somebody I wanted to emulate. He was captain and played in the famous No 13 shirt at Wigan and I wanted to do the same for Leeds."

Sinfield made a flying start as skipper, leading Rhinos to victory in their opening 10 league and cup games. The most famous of those was a classic Challenge Cup semi-final against St Helens at Huddersfield, now rated as one of the finest and most exciting games the historic competition has ever seen.

Beaten by Saints at the same stage in each of the two previous seasons, Leeds seemed to be on the verge of more semi-final agony when Darren Smith scored a try to put the Merseysiders 26-20 ahead with just three minutes remaining.

The conversion could have opened a two-score gap and sent Saints through to the final, but crucially Paul Sculthorpe's kick was off target, giving Rhinos one last chance.

A Saints knock-on and then a penalty put Leeds on their opponents' goalline and youngster Danny McGuire made the pressure count, throwing a dummy and nipping over at the corner to narrow the gap to two points.

The try was scored tight to the right-hand touchline, giving Sinfield – a right-footed kicker - the toughest-possible task, but he nailed the conversion to level the scores and send the tie into extra time. Thirteen years later Sinfield was to land an equally important kick, from almost the same spot, as Leeds staged another astonishing rally en-route to winning the league leaders' shield.

The drama continued as Saints had a touchdown disallowed before Sinfield edged Rhinos ahead with a drop goal and he

ENEMIES BEFORE PALS...Kevin Sinfield
and Jamie Peacock were to become
outstanding friends and teammates, but
in 2002 they were in opposite camps.

LAYING DOWN THE LAW...Even in his first year as captain Kevin
Sinfield was not afraid to stamp his authority, as on this occasion
during a defeat by Bradford Bulls at Odsal.

then converted another McGuire try to seal a sensational 33-26 triumph. Afterwards, Rhinos chief executive Gary Hetherington described Sinfield's equalising goal, with the final kick of normal time, as the most important in the club's history.

Just two weeks after the high against St Helens came one of the deepest lows of Sinfield's Leeds career, a 22-20 loss to Bradford Bulls in the Challenge Cup final at Cardiff's Millennium Stadium. Hailed as one of the heroes of the semi-final, Sinfield was blamed for the defeat, in the first rugby league game to be played below a closed roof, after opting not to go for goal from a late penalty which could have levelled the scores.

Rhinos were trailing by two points with time ebbing away, but Sinfield – who had already landed four goals from as many attempts - decided to keep the pressure on and go for a winning touchdown, rather than possibly settling for a draw and a replay at Elland Road. Leeds threw everything they had at their West Yorkshire rivals' defence, but Bulls held out to record their second big match win over Leeds in four seasons and inflict the first of what was to be five Cup final defeats for Sinfield.

"It was tough," Sinfield said of his decision not to kick for goal with the late penalty, which is something fans still argue about now. "You do what you think is right at the time. I felt at the time Bradford were tired. We'd had a lot of pressure on them and I thought they were ready to crack. At that stage I had only been kicking full-time since the start of the season and it wasn't an easy kick. The ones from the sidelines, like in the semi-final, there's less pressure on because people don't necessarily expect you to get them. I felt we had them at the time and we opted to run it, but they held out. It is history now, but I certainly got a lot of stick for it after the game."

It was a tough afternoon all round for Leeds, with coach Powell claiming afterwards that "every 50-50 decision" had gone against his

HIS GREATEST GOAL?...Danny McGuire's last-gasp try left Leeds two points adrift in the 2003 Challenge Cup semi-final. Kevin Sinfield's conversion from the touchline sent the tie into extra-time.

MAGSY MAGIC...Danny McGuire burst on to the scene with two tries
in Rhinos' 2003 Challenge Cup semi-final win over St Helens.

CRUNCH...Bradford Bulls knocked the stuffing out of Leeds - and their captain - several times in 2003, including the Challenge Cup final.

side. A crucial turning point came in the first half when Rob Burrow was introduced off the bench, but lasted just two minutes before being concussed in a tackle by Lee Gilmour. Powell had opted not to select semi-final hero McGuire and Leeds, reduced to 16 fit players, lacked a game-breaker among their substitutes.

There's an old saying that what doesn't kill you makes you stronger. Sinfield is a firm believer in that. He added: "Having missed out in 2000 it was my first final and to not only lose, but also get a lot of criticism was tough, but again it is probably part of the resilience I have now and that character you build up over the years. It makes you a bit thick-skinned and it was another one to get up off the canvas from."

Initially the Cardiff setback did not seem to knock Rhinos off course. It was Leeds' only defeat in their opening 15 games of 2003 and by late June they had lost just twice in 20 league and cup matches, but then the wheels came off. Rhinos slipped to second in the Super League table and lost both their play-offs ties, becoming the first top-two team not to reach the Grand Final. Bradford, who had finished top, beat Wigan at Old Trafford and their Leeds-born forward Jamie Peacock was named Man of Steel, as the year's most impressive individual.

A factor in Rhinos' slump was the loss of two rising stars, Chev Walker and Ryan Bailey, who were sentenced to time in custody over their involvement in an incident on a night out in Leeds. It was a unique situation for the club and players, who took time out from training to visit their teammates behind bars.

"It was a sad and difficult time for everybody," Sinfield said. "I am not condoning what they did, but it was tough seeing two of your mates going through that and they were top players, so a big part of our team was missing. The way the club stood by them was outstanding and Gary and Daryl deserve a lot of credit. Young people make mistakes, but I think they were made an example of because of their high profile."

Top: WINNER AND LOSER...Leeds' Gary Connolly picked up the 2003 Lance Todd Trophy, but that did not make up for the pain of a Cup final defeat.

Bottom: THANKING THE FANS...Chris McKenna shows his despair as Kevin Sinfield applauds Leeds' supporters after the first rugby league game staged in Cardiff's Millennium Stadium.

INDOOR RUGBY...Rhinos' 2003 Cup final defeat to Bradford at Cardiff's Millennium Stadium was the first rugby league game played under a closed roof.

Sinfield also felt a long year took its toll. Rhinos' Great Britain contingent, including the captain, went straight from Test duty into pre-season on an Army camp in Germany. They then had a short break before resuming preparations for the new season and battled through the entire campaign without a free weekend. The long build-up may have contributed to their strong start, but also the way they ran out of steam at the business end.

Despite the disappointing manner in which the 2003 season ended, it was a year of progress for Sinfield personally. His debut campaign as captain was the first in which he finished as Rhinos' leading points and goal scorer and broke through the 100 goals mark. He repeated those achievements every season for the rest of his rugby league career.

From a club point of view, in the second half of 2003 it was clear Rhinos were on the verge of winning silverware, but needed an x-factor to bridge the gap from contenders to champions. The solution as far as Gary Hetherington was concerned lay a few miles west along the M62, in Huddersfield.

On July 30 Rhinos announced that Tony Smith, Giants' Australian head coach, was to join them at the end of the season, with Powell becoming director of rugby. Powell later had a spell in rugby union coaching at Leeds Carnegie before returning to league with Featherstone Rovers and then Castleford Tigers and also having a part-time stint on the national team's backroom staff. Powell was in charge of Leeds for less than three full seasons, but Sinfield believes he deserves recognition for sowing the seeds which were to sprout into the success achieved during Rhinos' golden decade.

"He was very honest," Sinfield said of his former teammate turned boss. "He is very, very smart and an absolute gentleman, a really nice bloke and a very good coach as well. It doesn't surprise me what a good coach he has turned into. Some of the work he did with England was brilliant and I really enjoyed playing under him. He was fresh and innovative and he wanted to give young lads a chance. A lot of us blossomed under his coaching. We were very close in 2003 and I would like to think had Daryl stayed we would have won some trophies in 2004."

IN THE NEWS...The 2003 Challenge Cup semi-final classic against St Helens made headlines on the front and back pages of The Yorkshire Evening Post.

GOING FOR WARD...Jamie Peacock, pictured (right) tackling Danny Ward, won the Challenge Cup twice for Bradford against Leeds, the second time being at Cardiff in 2003.

BECOMING A HABIT...Rhinos and their fans suffered a second defeat in as many Cup finals at Cardiff in 2003.

BIG MAC, NO FRIES...Barrie McDermott was one of Kevin Sinfield's closest pals during his early days at Leeds. 'Baz' won this particular contest.

BRIGHT FUTURE...Chev Walker and Danny McGuire were two of Rhinos' most exciting home-grown talents in 2003.

GORED BY BULLS...Mark Calderwood and Danny McGuire reflect on Rhinos' defeat at Bradford in the 2003 play-offs.

HEAD TO HEAD...Rhinos lost to Bradford Bulls, who were captained by Robbie Paul, five times in 2003, including a Super League play-off semi-final.

HEARTBREAK...Leeds' 2003 season ended with a one-point play-offs loss to Wigan at Headingley. Wayne McDonald consoles a devastated Willie Poching.

CHAPTER FOUR
UP AND BACK DOWN
2004-2006

Leeds Rhinos had the time of their life in 2004. Under new coach Tony Smith they won 24 of their 28 games in the regular Super League season, with just two defeats and a brace of draws.

They finished nine points clear of Bradford Bulls at the top of the table, the first time Leeds had achieved that feat since 1972, and scored 1,037 points in the process, conceding a miserly 443. Rhinos went on to reach their second Grand Final at Old Trafford, where a 16-8 victory over Bradford secured their maiden Super League title and meant Leeds were champions for the first time in 32 years.

In his second season as captain Sinfield was a key component of Leeds' first Grand Final-winning squad, scoring 323 points, including 155 goals, in 31 appearances; but he credits Smith with turning them into a team of winners.

"He came in with a totally different approach," Sinfield recalled of the former Huddersfield boss. "We went right back to basics. He was very hard working and diligent and very determined, just a cracking all-round bloke and coach.

"I hit it off with him straight away and really enjoyed playing under him. You could tell from the off he wasn't going to accept second-best from anybody. He created a fantastic environment where it was all about improving every day."

Leeds didn't quite have it all their own way that year. A 24-16 defeat at St Helens in the fifth round of the Challenge Cup was a savage blow at the time, but proved a blessing in disguise as it meant Rhinos had three free weekends before the end of the league campaign.

Rhinos' second defeat of the year was also at Knowsley Road, a 56-10 hammering, but they gained spectacular revenge with a 70-0 win in the Headingley return. They scored 40 or more points 14 times in all competitions and Sinfield said: "Our skill level was as good as it has ever been and that was down to the hard work put in by Tony and Brian McDermott, who was his assistant.

"We had a very young team, but a very good one and the style of rugby we played in some of those games was unbelievable. I remember really enjoying the games and that's probably why we did so well. We got the best out of each other."

Top try scorer for Rhinos that year was Danny McGuire, with 39. Sinfield added: "Magsy thrived, because we made so many breaks. There's nobody in the game better at supporting and finishing tries off.

"He was outstanding and it was a shame he didn't get Man of Steel. Rob Burrow and Matt Diskin both had a top year as well. All the young guys who had come through the system stepped up and I would like to make special mention of Willie Poching, who made a fantastic contribution off the bench."

WHERE'S YOUR TIE?...This group of players and staff won Leeds' first Championship for 32 years. They are pictured at the club's awards night.

ALI THE GREAT...The mid-season signing of Ali Lauitiiti, shown here arriving in Leeds and in typical action against Wigan, was crucial as Leeds dominated Super League in 2004.

BLESSING IN DISGUISE...Barrie McDermott and Ryan Bailey and Marcus Bai and Gary Connolly were left devastated by Rhinos' 2004 Challenge Cup defeat at St Helens, but things worked out well in the end.

GOOD BAI...Marcus Bai joined Leeds in 2004 and became the first Papua New Guinean to play for the club. His 26 tries that year included this one against St Helens.

RECORD BREAKER...Danny McGuire scored 39 tries in 30 appearances during 2004. This one against Wakefield set a new record for the most touchdowns in a Super League season.

LEAGUE LEADERS...Rhinos topped the table for the first time in 32 years in 2004. Barrie McDermott and Kevin Sinfield enjoyed the moment after the trophy presentation, along with their teammates.

COACH AND CAPTAIN...Tony Smith, celebrating at Old Trafford, turned Rhinos from nearly-men into winners.

YOU BEAUTY...Kevin Sinfield lifts the Super League trophy for the first time, in 2004.

CHAMPIONS AT LAST...Thirty two years is a long time between drinks. Rhinos' players celebrated in appropriate fashion after claiming the Super League trophy for the first time.

Rhinos also had the luxury of recruiting ball-handling forward Ali Lauitiiti from New Zealand Warriors as a mid-season signing. He bolstered an already very strong team and Sinfield said: "I remember being dazzled by his skills.

"He was something else, a basketballer in a rugby player's body. He was quick and aggressive, but always smiling and a dream to play with. He was a terrific signing; he lifted the team when he came in and was a big catalyst for us going on and winning the comp."

The league leaders' shield was secured on a memorable night at Headingley, in August, 2004, when relegation-bound Castleford Tigers were crushed 64-12. Leeds had a scare in their opening play-offs tie, losing 26-12 at home to Bradford, but a 40-12 drubbing of Wigan in the final eliminator secured a return to Old Trafford for the first time since 1998.

Of the 17 players on duty in the Grand Final, only David Furner had been alive the previous time Leeds won the championship. "It was huge," Sinfield said of the title decider. "There was a lot of pressure on us and we were all aware of the chokers tag the club had carried for 32 years.

"There was a huge expectation that we would win the Grand Final, but given the fact we had a young team and the way we'd dropped off the year before, we were very wary. The play-off defeat to Bradford at home was probably the wake-up call we needed.

"Though it encouraged the doubters to doubt even more, it actually gave us a steely belief. If we'd beaten Bradford we would have had a week off before the Grand Final and I don't think that would have worked in our favour. We were a team who liked to play every week at that stage. Tony handled things really well, he knew people expected us to choke, but he held things together."

Smith's ruthless streak was crucial to Leeds' success, according to Sinfield. "For the Wigan play-off game he dropped Andrew Dunemann and Matt Adamson and I think that signalled what he was all about. He wasn't afraid to make changes if he felt that was the right thing for the team. That caused some collateral damage, but when you go on and win it is hard to say the coach has made the wrong call.

"On the other hand, he brought Jamie Jones-Buchanan into the team after the Bradford game. He was the first coach to put any trust in Jonesy and he instilled a belief that's still there today. He created, through giving him the nod in those two games, something that has lasted more than 10 years."

The Grand Final was a tense affair and hung in the balance until five minutes from time when McGuire crossed for a try which Sinfield converted.

"That was a moment of absolute joy," Sinfield said of McGuire's touchdown. "It was my first major trophy and I can remember the trip back from Manchester, with Green Day's 'Time of Your Life' on the bus's sound system.

"Those are the special moments and memories you keep with you. There was a bit of relief, but a whole lot of satisfaction because of the way we had played and proved the doubters wrong. That was the start of it and it gave some young players a taste of how good winning a Grand Final is. Once you've tasted it you get greedy and you want to go back."

Out of a crowd of 65,537, one individual's presence at the Grand Final made it even more special for Sinfield. "My son Jack was born three weeks before and it was his first game. That was nice."

The win at Old Trafford set-up a World Club Challenge showdown with Australian champions Canterbury Bulldogs to kick off the 2005 season. A huge crowd of 37,028 saw Rhinos stun the Aussies 39-32 at Leeds United's Elland Road stadium, thanks largely to a man of the match performance from Sinfield, who kicked six goals and a drop.

CATCH ME IF YOU CAN...Kevin Sinfield bursts past Bradford captain Jamie Peacock in 2005. The two became teammates the following year.

RHINOS UNITED...Leeds' players rush to help Richard Mathers celebrate his
World Club Challenge try against Canterbury Bulldogs at Elland Road.

HERO WORSHIP...Ellery Hanley was the young Kevin Sinfield's rugby league idol. In 2005 Hanley presented the Leeds captain with Super League's April player of the month award.

Rhinos opened the campaign with eight straight wins and lost only three of their first 29 matches in all competitions, before defeats in five of their last seven, including 25-24 to Hull in the Challenge Cup final and 15-6 by Bradford at Old Trafford. They were also second in the league, completing an unwanted treble.

Despite that, Sinfield said: "I think we played some of our best rugby that year, even better than 2004. I wasn't selected for the internationals at the end of 2004 so I'd had six weeks at home with my wife-to-be Jayne and our first born and then I had my first full pre-season as a professional. That was great for me and I went into 2005 absolutely bouncing.

"It was certainly one of my best years. I was up for Man of Steel, along with Jamie Lyon and Jamie Peacock and I got the Lance Todd Trophy [as man of the match in the Challenge Cup final], even though we lost.

"Some of the rugby we played that year was unreal. The World Club was a very strange game, we were miles in front and they came back at us. Everyone remembers Sonny Bill Williams' shot on Marcus Bai, but we held on. That was the first World Championship for us and it was a really special night."

Making his debut against Canterbury was back-rower Gareth Ellis, who had been signed from Wakefield Trinity Wildcats. Sinfield and Ellis were the same school age and had crossed paths at amateur and academy level before hitting the big time.

"He's a cracking lad," Sinfield said. "When he came to Leeds that year he flourished. I think people are still shuddering from some of the tackles he made. He is right up there with players I've played with. He was great in the dressing room, very good for team spirit and a fantastic player. He was tough, skilful and he had magic feet for a big man. I was gutted when he left [at the end of 2008] to join Wests Tigers. I thought we missed a trick there because he was such a good player."

Looking back on 2005 is a bitter-sweet experience for Sinfield, given it was a case of so near, yet so far for the defending champions. He said: "We started the year on fire, but the Challenge Cup final hurt. We wanted to make things right after 2003, but Hull did a job on us. They held us down all day and they stopped us from playing.

"To lose by a point was very, very tough and then to have to collect the Lance Todd Trophy on the pitch wasn't something I really wanted to do. Not at any stage was having that trophy a consolation, though now I can look back and it is something I am proud of.

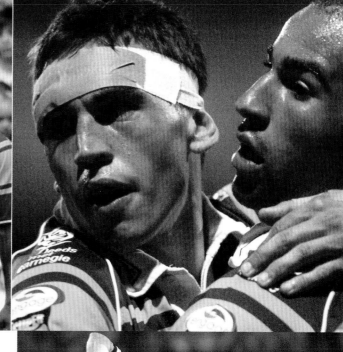

DOWN AND OUT...Hull inflicted Kevin Sinfield's second Challenge Cup final defeat, in 2005. Worse was to follow.

CHIN UP: Kevin Sinfield consoles Marcus Bai after Rhinos conceded a try to Hull in the 2005 Challenge Cup final.

BLOODY MARVELLOUS...Kevin Sinfield, celebrating a try with Chev Walker, went through some tough times as Leeds came up short in 2005.

HAVING A BALL...Gareth Ellis was a major signing for Rhinos in 2005.

GOODBYE AND HELLO...Jamie Peacock's final game for Bradford was their 2005 Grand Final win over Leeds, the team he was about to join.

PIES COOKED...Rhinos hit back from 16 points down to win 24-16 at Wigan early in 2006, Sinfield scoring the try which edged them ahead.

OUCH...Kevin Sinfield suffered serious knee and ankle injuries in a 2006 win at Hull. That led to a lengthy spell on the sidelines, including this game at Salford (right). Chris Feather was another casualty at the time.

LAYING DOWN THE LAW...Sinfield was back in action when Rhinos returned to Hull late in the season. A 23-16 defeat proved costly.

MUD GLORIOUS MUD...Kevin Sinfield was among the try scorers when Rhinos defied awful conditions to beat Leigh 36-12 in a 2006 Challenge Cup tie at Hilton Park.

"Then losing in the Grand Final was hugely disappointing. That year I think perhaps we just ran out of steam. When we got to Old Trafford our momentum was slowing and Bradford's was getting better and better.

"Their coach Brian Noble was under pressure and they brought in Adrian Morley just for the play-offs. As we showed in 2011 and 2012, if you are a good side and you get momentum at that stage of the season you can be very difficult to stop. On the night they were too good."

Bradford were captained by Jamie Peacock in his final game for them before joining Leeds. He was also Great Britain skipper and Sinfield regards Peacock as the best signing Rhinos have made in the Super League era and possibly ever.

"He had just snatched the trophy off us, but he was a Leeds lad and as soon as he came in you could tell all he wanted to do was play for Leeds," Sinfield said. "If it wasn't for JP we wouldn't have won all the trophies we have over the past 10 years. To bring someone with his experience and leadership into the club was great work by Tony and Gary. Although 2006 was a tough year for us, we certainly got the best out of JP in the years after that. He is a fantastic friend and one of the two best players I have played with, the other one being Jamie Jones-Buchanan."

Though Peacock was a star addition, Rhinos actually took a step back in 2006. They suffered a shock Challenge Cup semi-final loss to Huddersfield Giants, finished third in Super League and were beaten by Warrington Wolves in their opening play-off. With things going that badly, the finger was pointed at Sinfield and his relationship with Peacock. There were rumours of unrest between the pair, but Sinfield is adamant none of that was true.

"I can understand why people might think that," he admitted. "JP was Great Britain captain and had been captain of Bradford, but he was brilliant. If at any stage in the pre-season Tony had come to me and said JP was the man to take the team forward, I would have been really

disappointed, but I'd have accepted it. I knew what JP was about, I had been captained by him at international level and I was just delighted we'd signed him.

"I wanted to work with him and if that had meant being his vice-captain or just as a general team member, I would have got on with my job and done it the best I could. But Tony never mentioned anything like that to me. He stood by me and I have to say, I don't think JP expected it.

"He was desperate to play for his hometown club and win trophies here. I am sure he would have taken it if he had been offered it, he would have been a fool not to, but at no stage did I feel threatened by him. That's a big credit to JP and to have him in our dressing room was fantastic."

CHAPTER FIVE
A TEST OF CHARACTER
2000-2013

Kevin Sinfield made a Mickey Mouse start to his international career, his first England appearance coming at Disneyland Resort in Florida in a huge win over the United States.

That was a warm-up to the 2000 World Cup and Sinfield was a substitute in England's opening defeat to Australia at Twickenham for his first proper taste of Test rugby.

His maiden start was in England's second game, a 76-4 thrashing of Russia at St Helens' Knowsley Road, when he scored what was to be the only hat-trick of his professional career.

He was back on the bench for the hosts' final group game, against Fiji at Headingley, but left out of England's quarter-final and semi-final teams.

England were thrashed by New Zealand in the last four and – remarkably - Sinfield's treble against Russia meant he finished the tournament as their joint-second leading try scorer, level with Wigan's Tony Smith and three behind Jamie Peacock.

The tournament is remembered as a disaster, financially and for England, but from Sinfield's point of view it was "really, really positive".

He said: "We had quite a young team and it was great to be involved."

Sinfield's full Great Britain debut was away to France in 2001 and he also featured in that year's Ashes, when Australia bounced back from defeat in the opening Test to win the series 2-1.

"In the first game I was named at hooker, but played at scrum-half, the first time I had ever played there," he recalled.

"It was a brilliant occasion to beat Australia. The crowd at Huddersfield that night was immense. We got hammered in the second Test, at Bolton, but the third was at Wigan and it was very close. We were desperately unlucky, as we were in a number of Tests against the Aussies during my time."

The following year England visited Australia for a one-off, mid-season Test in Sydney. Sinfield is probably the only Great Britain player who has fond memories of the trip, which culminated in a record 64-10 defeat.

"We were there for five days and got a hammering in the Test," he said. "But I came off the bench and scored my first and only try for Great Britain. It was my first time in Australia and I was excited about seeing a bit of the world. Our hotel was based on Manly beach, which was a great spot and it was an enjoyable trip, apart from the result."

Great Britain regained some pride that autumn when they hit back from a game down to draw a home series with New

YOUNG GUNS...Kevin Sinfield in England Schools action against France. Jamie Jones-Buchanan and Leeds' Gary Smith and George Rayner also featured. The year was 1997.

Zealand, Sinfield playing in the first and second Tests, but there was more disappointment against the Aussies in 2003. England were whitewashed 3-0, but actually went agonisingly close to their first Ashes series win since 1970.

"In every game we were winning until the final 20 minutes," remembered Sinfield, who came off the bench in the second and third Tests. "It was really disappointing not to at least get one win, but I think it showed how we had closed the gap on Australia.

"We probably didn't have that belief to go on and get the results in the end. It wasn't fitness, but I think they truly believed in their game plan and came up with it."

Sinfield was dropped from the international scene in 2004, recalled for the following year's home Tri-Nations campaign and missed the 2006 tour Down Under due to a knee injury.

By 2007 Tony Smith, the departing Leeds boss, was in charge of England and he recalled Sinfield for a 3-0 series victory against the touring Kiwis, which was to prove Sinfield's only tournament win over southern hemisphere opposition.

Sinfield said: "I had to pull out of the first game. I was sick through the night at the hotel, got up in the morning and declared myself fit and then was sick again on the team walk, in Leeds. As soon as that happened I was ruled out. I played in the second game, in Hull and then didn't play in the third."

ULTIMATE TEST...Kevin Sinfield's international career lasted 13 years. He was a member of England's 2000 World Cup squad, along with Rhinos' Adrian Morley, Andy Hay, Keith Senior, Francis Cummins, Darren Fleary and Chev Walker, while Barrie McDermott, Senior and Gary Connolly lined up against Australia for Great Britain in 2003.

Being left out of the final Test denied Sinfield an opportunity to play in Great Britain's final match before the home nations were split into four separate teams, but he went into the 2008 World Cup in Australia on the back of Leeds having retained their Super League title with a second successive Grand Final victory over St Helens.

The two big guns provided 15 of England's 24-man touring party, just weeks after their Old Trafford showdown. England lost three of their four matches and unrest between Leeds and Saints players was widely blamed for their dismal campaign.

"I don't necessarily think that was the case," Sinfield insisted. "I just don't think we spent enough time with each other."

Sinfield featured in England's opening game, a nervy win over Papua New Guinea and kept his place for the other group matches against Australia and New Zealand, but was left out of their semi-final loss to the Kiwis.

He revealed: "It was a tough trip to be on. Sam, our second son, was about eight months old and he spent a fair bit of time in hospital while I was over in Australia. So not only had I been left out of the team, he was poorly 12,000 miles away."

That tournament was a watershed in Sinfield's international career. He had been playing – on and off – at Test level for eight years, but had yet to establish himself as a regular starter or hit the heights he had reached in a Leeds shirt.

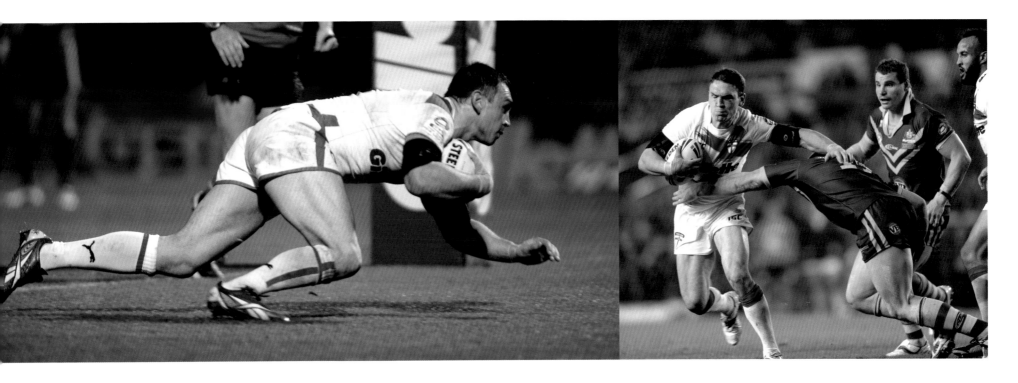

RECORD BREAKER...Kevin Sinfield is England's record points scorer.

International duty inevitably meant a late finish to the playing year and missing out on the important early stages of pre-season with Rhinos and Sinfield admitted, after another disappointing World Cup, he came close to calling it quits.

"I remember flying home from Australia at the end of 2008 thinking 'this isn't going to happen for me'," he said. "I thought that either I wasn't good enough, or the quality of people in my position - Andy Farrell and Paul Sculthorpe were outstanding in my early years at international level - meant it would be tough for me to get into the team.

"The style of play we used under various coaches possibly didn't suit my build at that stage; I just wasn't big enough to play in the positions I was being asked to. Sam was poorly at home, I had sacrificed a lot and I wasn't particularly getting

anything back in return.

"Not that you should in international rugby; you are prepared to make those sacrifices to represent your country, but though there had been some good times on tour, I wasn't really enjoying my rugby. You get the best out of me when I am enjoying it and that wasn't happening. I came close to saying 'that's it with internationals', but then in 2009 things got a whole lot better."

Smith recalled Sinfield for England's opening win over France, at Doncaster and he remained in the starting team throughout the Four Nations series, which ended with defeat by Australia in a pulsating final at Elland Road.

Smith resigned as coach after that loss and Steve McNamara took over, a change which suited the Rhinos skipper. "2010 was the first year when I really felt wanted and part of it. I think I played my best international rugby under Steve Mac, even though Tony had been my club coach. Under Tony, for whatever reason, it didn't work out, but I am glad I stuck with international rugby.

"I really enjoyed playing under Steve and the way he wanted us to play and the environment he created. He brought in a change of culture. Up to then there had been club cliques and certain players didn't get on, but that all changed under Steve. He tried to break all that down and get us to enjoy each other's company.

"He came up with a philosophy of playing for two teams, rather than one club. I think that worked really well and we saw the fruits of that with England's Test series win over the Kiwis in 2015."

England finished third in the 2010 Four Nations and were runners-up the following year, again losing to Australia in the final at Elland Road. Sinfield played at stand-off in that series, alongside Castleford Tigers' Rangi Chase and was favourite to take over as skipper after Peacock announced he was stepping down.

"In 2011 we won the Grand Final and I won the Harry Sunderland award [as man of the match]. Two days later Steve gave me the captain's job and that was probably the best week of my career," Sinfield reflected.

"It was something I had dreamed of from the time Ellery Hanley was Great Britain captain. Seeing him lead the team out and wear the No 13 shirt, that was something I always wanted to do.

"At 32 I thought it had passed me by. JP's international retirement surprised me, but it opened the door. I felt so, so fortunate to be given that role and I really enjoyed it. The culture we had started to create fitted in with the club environment at Leeds."

Sinfield led England to victory in a home tri-series against France and Wales and wore the armband for his third World Cup, in 2013; something he described as a "huge honour."

He said, "It was an unbelievable experience, it came with its challenges, but it was very enjoyable and very tough, especially the way it ended."

Sinfield's last international appearance was a World Cup semi-final against New Zealand at Wembley, in November 2013. The tie, which the Kiwis won 20-18 thanks to Shaun Johnson's last-minute try, has been described as one of

the finest games in international rugby league's history, but that is still no consolation to England's captain.

"I think it was my best-ever appearance for England," Sinfield said. "We played so well and lost it in the last few seconds. I shot out of the line to put pressure on Shaun Johnson, which was something we had talked about: moving up and getting rid of his space.

"He had a wicked sidestep and the next thing was a bit of a blur, because we were under the posts and we knew we were going out. It was horrendous, I remember travelling back up north on the coach and I wasn't ready to go home.

"I had missed home for about five weeks, but I just wasn't ready to go back. The whole week after that was a blur; I was there physically, but not mentally.

"You feel like you have let a lot of people down, but it was a great advert for our game and I think it lit a few flames for international rugby league and showed we weren't far away.

"What made it worse was how the Kiwis played in the final. They got hammered by Australia and I do think we would have given a better account of ourselves."

Sinfield announced his international retirement almost a year later, following a much happier Wembley experience. He finally got his hands on the Challenge Cup in August, 2014, after Rhinos defeated neighbours Castleford and he broke the news to his international colleagues a few days later.

He said: "On the way back from the World Cup semi-final I spoke to Steve McNamara and asked if it was time for me to step down and move on. He said no and I remember James Graham and a few of the other boys texting me to say the same, which was great of them.

"I think if there had been a mid-season Test that year I would have made myself available. That might have prevented me from retiring, but I had more time to think about it and more time out of the camp.

"I had time to evaluate where I was and also I think England were in a great place, with some quality players coming through. The next goal was to win the 2017 World Cup and the best way to give ourselves a chance of doing that was by blooding some young players and giving them a chance every year.

"It was the right call for me and for the team. Sometimes you can stay around for too long, but I feel very fortunate to have played so many times for my country and to have been captain as well.

"I am really glad I stuck with it after 2008 and although the semi-final defeat by the Kiwis still hurts, I am really proud of how we played."

CHAPTER SIX
A KIND OF MAGIC
2007

At the start of the 2007 season it seemed Leeds Rhinos' lone Super League triumph might have been a flash in the pan.

Three years earlier they had looked set for a period of dominance under coach Tony Smith, but in 2005 Rhinos finished runners-up in all three domestic competitions and the following season was an even bigger disappointment as they failed to qualify for either Wembley or Old Trafford.

Smith's fourth campaign as coach proved to be his last, but it was also the start of a remarkable, record-breaking run during which Rhinos won three successive Grand Finals, all against 2006's treble winners St Helens.

Leeds were in the mix throughout 2007, but it was only the final two months of the regular season when they emerged as genuine title contenders. By that stage Smith had already dropped a bombshell, announcing in March he would be leaving at the end of the year to take over as Great Britain boss.

"It was a bit of a shock," Kevin Sinfield said of Smith's decision to leave club coaching. "But given Tony's coaching ability, when the Great Britain job came up for grabs he was the obvious choice and probably the only choice at the time."

Rather like what was to happen eight years later, the impending departure of a key member of Leeds' set-up provided added motivation, though it took a while for that to

have an impact and there were times during the year when a section of fans called for Smith to step down early, because of disappointing results.

"We wanted to send Tony off in the right way," Sinfield recalled. "That meant a lot to us because he had got our first trophy, in 2004, but until the back end it wasn't a great year for us. Mentally we found it very, very tough and there were some good sides out there.

"We probably didn't play as well as we should have for a lot of the year, but it all came together in the end. With the way Super League was and the play-offs format, if you got some momentum at the right time you could go on and win it and that's what we did."

Two key signings made a huge contribution to Leeds' title triumph. Brent Webb came in from New Zealand Warriors and was Rhinos' top try scorer with 24, including one in the Grand Final conquering of St Helens.

"He was the best full-back in the world at the time," Sinfield stated. "Billy Slater was a different type of full-back, very much a running type and Darren Lockyer was still around, but had transformed into a stand-off.

"Webby came in and he was unbelievable, he transformed the modern full-back role. Before he came over full-backs were either runners or ball-players, but he was both. He had

ON THE UP...Ryan Hall was a member of Leeds' 2007 Academy Grand Final-winning side. A year later he added his first Super League winner's ring.

MAGIC MOMENT...Jordan Tansey's try secured victory for Leeds against Bradford at the 2007 Magic Weekend - and caused uproar.

WE LOVE YOU SENIOR...Keith Senior was one of the world's best centres during a glittering career with Rhinos from 1999-2011.

brilliant skills and he was a great bloke to have around the dressing room; he really added to the mix."

As did Rhinos' front-row signing from Manly Sea Eagles, Kylie Leuluai. The Samoan international had been a journeyman in the NRL, but found a home at Leeds and went on to become the club's most successful overseas recruit.

Said Sinfield: "Kylie was one of the best players I have ever played with and there is no better bloke around. He became such a fantastic talisman for us. He was a role model for me in many ways; he has a great family, he is a thoughtful bloke and a real leader. He didn't say a lot, but when he did speak everyone listened.

"He was a bit of a smiling assassin, when he hit someone they knew they had been hit. If somebody took liberties or crossed the line, you could tell from his eyes what was coming. His retribution was ferocious, but in a legal way. He was a great signing for us."

A third Rhinos great, Ryan Hall, emerged in 2007, making his debut in the most controversial game Super League has ever seen. The first Magic Weekend was staged during Super League XII, when an entire round of matches were staged over two days at Cardiff's Millennium Stadium.

Rhinos' derby with Bradford Bulls was chosen to close the event and it proved to be an explosive finale. Bulls led 38-36 with seconds left when Rhinos were awarded a penalty, incorrectly as replays later showed, on the intervention of video official Ashley Klein.

Sinfield took a shot at goal, his kick rebounded off the crossbar and Jordan Tansey followed up to touch down as the hooter sounded. Referee Steve Ganson awarded the try without asking for Klein's help and the captain converted to seal an incredible 42-38 success.

That was dramatic enough, but controversy exploded when replays clearly showed Tansey had been standing in front of Sinfield when the kick was taken and was therefore offside. Had Ganson passed the decision on to his video assistant the try would have been ruled out, handing victory to Bulls.

"We didn't play particularly well," is Sinfield's opinion of Leeds' performance that evening. "We were really frustrated with our performance, but we got the penalty late on, 40 metres out and I remember there were a couple of their lads having a chirp, trying to put me off.

"But a couple of them were upset with Steve Ganson, I could hear the expletives aimed at him and I think what happened next was a bit of a reaction to that. I think the verbals he was getting influenced his decision not to go to the screen. It is an example of why you should keep the referee on your side and always be respectful and polite to the officials. There's no doubt we got lucky and got out of jail.

"It will go down in history; people still talk about it now and I can understand why Leeds fans enjoyed it so much, against the old enemy who had caused us so much pain over the years. I have got no idea what Jordan Tansey was doing setting off like he did, but looking back now, it was quite funny!"

TOP TRIO...Sinfield celebrates with Rob Burrow and Danny McGuire against Hull in 2007. The three were at the heart of Rhinos' success that season.

Sinfield's unique celebration after Tansey's try is something he has never lived down. "I did an infamous cartwheel," he recalled. "I am not sure where that came from, but I was just so excited about going from having lost the game, to maybe drawing it and then actually coming away with the win. I didn't realise Jordan was offside until I saw the replays afterwards."

Raging Bulls were, understandably, furious, even going as far as asking Leeds to hand back the two points. Sinfield added: "Steve McNamara was in charge of Bradford and he is the best international coach I have played under.

"We get on really well, but I remember him taking the England job in 2010 and still being a bit frosty with me because of that, like it was my fault it happened! We have laughed about it since, but it is still pretty raw with Steve."

Rhinos went on to finish second in Super League, with Bulls four points behind in third, so the notorious Cardiff showdown had a major influence on the table, but it also left a lasting legacy. Ashley Gibson was ruled out with what proved to be a season-ending knee injury, so young winger Ryan Hall was drafted in among the substitutes for his senior debut.

"He came from nowhere," Sinfield said of the future international, who had been signed from community club Oulton Raiders' open-age team. "In the 2006 off-season I didn't go on tour because of a knee problem so I got a full pre-season in. This young, skinny kid came in and we got paired off in training to do tackling work. He smashed me all over the field and I can remember thinking 'who is this'?

"Within a few months he had become very much part of the group and he was – and still is – different, but in a good way. He is very intelligent, he plays the piano and can do the

SUPERMAN...Full-back Brent Webb lived up to his fans' nickname by swooping over for Leeds' opening try in the 2007 title decider. Afterwards, he celebrated with the club's long-serving timekeeper Billy Watts.

THE GOLDEN MOMENT...Sinfield hoists the Super League trophy for the second time, at the end of the 2007 Grand Final.

Rubik's Cube and he is another player who contributed so much to our success.

"He has got speed and strength and I have never seen anyone who can deal with a high ball the way Hally can. He is known as the World's Best Winger and he deserves that; he is somebody who can break defences down and he scores tries that look impossible. His performance against Manly in 2013 went a long way towards us winning the World Club Challenge and over the next few years I can see him stepping up and really taking a leadership role in the team."

Bradford gained revenge for their Magic Weekend disappointment when they won 38-14 at Headingley the following month. That was the start of a run of three defeats in four games for Rhinos, culminating in a 23-16 home loss to Wakefield Trinity Wildcats.

A week after that derby embarrassment, Rhinos' title hopes appeared to be in tatters when they trailed 16-6 at half-time away to Harlequins, but that proved to be a turning point in their season. Leeds hit back in sensational style to win 54-20 and lost only two of their remaining eight matches.

The last of those was 10-8 at league leaders St Helens in a bruising play-off tie. Rhinos rebounded to thrash visitors Wigan Warriors 36-6 in the following week's final eliminator and set up an Old Trafford showdown with the defending champions. It was tight at the break, when Rhinos led 8-6, but Saints were blown away in the second half as Leeds ran out 33-6 victors to be crowned Super League champions for the second time.

"That Grand Final and the one in 2008 upset Saints' fans and players because they thought we had come from nowhere to take the title," Sinfield recalled. "They were outstanding in 2007 and I think they just ran out of steam.

"It was a bit like what Bradford did to us in 2005. We got into the play-offs and our momentum was speeding up and theirs was slowing down. There was a lot of emotion with it being

GLORY BOYS....Leeds went into the 2007 title decider as underdogs, but produced
a sensational all-round performance to beat league leaders St Helens 33-6.

Tony's last game and it was great to be part of a win like that.

"To be in a final with 20 minutes to go and know you have got it won, that doesn't happen very often, especially not against a quality side like Saints. To run up a score like that was absolutely brilliant, very, very pleasing."

The death of legendary former Leeds scrum half Jeff Stevenson was announced on the morning of the final, so it was fitting that No 7 Rob Burrow won the Harry Sunderland award as man of the match.

"Rob had a great year, capped by that performance," Sinfield said. "Rob and I came through the system together, though he is a couple of years younger than me and he has been a fantastic player for Leeds for a long time.

Left: MR VERSATILE...Lee Smith played in three Grand Finals for Rhinos, each in a different position and was a try scorer every time. This was in 2007.

Right: ALI UP...Ali Lauitiiti was among the try scorers when Leeds ripped St Helens apart at Old Trafford in 2007.

Opposite: THE 18TH MAN...Rhinos' supporters were in good spirits before, during and after the 2007 Super League Grand Final.

"He is a great person to have in the dressing room, he is very funny and he is one of those players who always really seems to step up in the big games. I have loved playing alongside Rob and Danny McGuire as well.

"They have both got the knack of coming up with crucial plays just when you need them and they are top club men; they have only ever wanted to play for Leeds and they have contributed so much over the years."

Sinfield kicked six goals in the rout of Saints, his opener making him the first man to play and score in every game of a season for Leeds. He finished the 32-match campaign with 305 points from six tries, 139 goals and three drop goals.

Victory in the title decider also wrote Smith into club history as the first coach to guide Leeds to two championship triumphs. Sinfield said: "He had a huge influence. Daryl Powell was brilliant and who knows what would have happened if he had still been in charge, but Tony, with his back to basics approach, transformed the club.

"He is a very good coach, very thorough and we learned something new every day. My relationship with him as captain and coach was brilliant and I feel very lucky to have spent four years playing under him. It was a very enjoyable time and successful as well."

BEARDED WONDER...Kevin Sinfield's best mate Jamie Jones-Buchanan scored the final try of 2007.

THE HULK...Kylie Leuluai joined Rhinos in 2007 and was at the heart of their success over the next nine years.

FATHER AND SON...Kevin and Jack Sinfield show off the trophy to a packed homecoming crowd at Headingley in 2007.

CHAPTER SEVEN
THE THREE-PEAT
2008-2010

As Leeds Rhinos coach, Tony Smith was a hard act to follow. Smith had been appointed to transform a talented young team into winners; his successor's task was to keep the trophies coming.

The man selected was Brian McClennan, known to everyone as Bluey. He arrived at Headingley with a big reputation from his time in charge of the New Zealand national side, having ended Australia's domination of Test rugby by winning the 2005 Tri-Nations final at Elland Road.

While Smith was respected as a brilliant technical coach, McClennan had made his name as a world-class motivator and he proved an ideal fit. Remarkably, by the time of his sudden exit in the autumn of 2010 McClennan had exactly matched his predecessor's achievements: two Grand Final wins, the league leaders' shield and world club title once each and a Challenge Cup final loss.

Reflecting on the impact McClennan made at Leeds, Kevin Sinfield said: "I am genuinely very, very fortunate to have played under some fantastic coaches and Bluey was one of them.

"He was massively enthusiastic and he loved the game. He was a huge family man and he had a great philosophy on the sport. We got on really well as captain and coach and I enjoyed my time playing under him."

Sinfield described McClennan as "probably the opposite of Tony", but felt that was what Rhinos needed at the time. He added: "He let the players have a lot more control and encouraged a culture of trying to share things and work through things together.

"He was also very smart and his rugby knowledge was outstanding. He would get his ideas across through history or a story and it worked really well. He was a gem of a bloke."

Rhinos won their first four Super League games under McClennan before taking on Australian champions Melbourne Storm in a ferocious World Club Challenge tussle at Elland Road. McClennan's men literally weathered the storm, defying both the opposition and horrendous conditions to win the title for the second time.

Sinfield, who booted three goals and a drop in Leeds' 11-4 triumph, despite having a laser pointed at him from the stand before one kick, remembered: "Bluey was completely focused on winning silverware, he believed that when you had an opportunity to do that you had to give it everything.

"The first four games we played were all about gearing up for Melbourne and he absolutely nailed it. The thing everyone remembers about that night was the weather, it was blowing a gale and when we came out for the warm-up I thought straightaway it was set up to be a big forward battle.

"Our conditioner Jason Davidson had put cones down and they were blowing all over the place. Those conditions might have suited Melbourne a bit more than us, because our style was built on free-flowing rugby, but on the night our pack was absolutely outstanding.

"We played a simple game plan, short balls, not putting the ball in the air for too long and it worked a treat. It was a really tough game, there were a record number of play-the-balls and to come through a game like that, against a good team like Melbourne and get the win was really pleasing."

Rhinos lost their next game, at lowly Castleford Tigers, but were beaten just twice in their opening 20 matches in all competitions. A mid-season wobble saw them lose five of their next eight, but they finished with a flourish.

St Helens, who had ended Rhinos' Wembley hopes at the semi-final stage of the Challenge Cup, finished top of the table for the fourth successive season, a point clear of the defending champions, who were second. When Rhinos were thrashed 38-10 at Knowsley Road in the play-offs it seemed Saints were set to regain the title, but a fortnight is a long time in rugby league.

Seven days after being embarrassed by Saints, Rhinos rallied to pip Wigan 18-14 in a tense elimination tie at Headingley. And 15 days after the semi-final setback they retained their crown with a stunning 24-16 conquering of the league leaders at Old Trafford.

"We were desperate to do well in the Challenge Cup that year and when Saints beat us in the semi-final it gave us even more motivation to get back to Old Trafford and hang

HATS OFF...Willie Poching, Matt Diskin and Jamie Jones-Buchanan weren't just teammates; they studied alongside Kevin Sinfield at Leeds Metropolitan University.

HARD TO HOLD...Ali Lauitiiti was a tough man to stop, even in training.

on to the trophy," Sinfield said.

"Having finished top again, Saints felt they were the best team and they felt they owed us one after 2007, but once you win a Grand Final it makes you hungry to do it again. We had that experience and we were a team that tended to play well on the big stage. Even after the game a couple of weeks earlier we knew if we performed we could cause Saints some problems and beat them for a second year."

Saints were hot favourites, but it was a night when things clicked into place for Leeds. Sinfield's highlight was Ryan Hall's first half try, scored from the rookie winger's own kick. Said the captain: "During the week Brent Webb hurt his back in training and had to pull out, so Lee Smith went to full-back and Hally was on the wing. Hally scored a great try and Lee was man of the match.

"It was another tough game, but to win the title two years running, under different coaches, was a great achievement. That is a tough thing to do in a salary cap sport and it illustrated what the whole club is about.

"When he came in Bluey didn't talk about defending the title because he thought that would make us the hunted rather than hunters. We talked about attacking it and we did that."

The following year was just as successful, though it began with disappointment when Rhinos' hopes of retaining the World Club Challenge were shattered by a 28-20 loss to Manly Sea Eagles at Elland Road.

"We were very well prepared, but for some reason it didn't happen for us," was Sinfield's assessment. "We weren't quite with it and they deserved to win on the night."

Rhinos made a shaky start to the year, including a home defeat by Saints in the Challenge Cup fourth round, before winning 17 of their final 19 games in all competitions. After Saints had led for much of the season Leeds overhauled them in August and finished four points clear at the top of the Super League table.

Like 2004, an early Cup loss - and some free weekends in mid-season - proved a blessing in disguise. But the easy way isn't the Leeds way and

WEATHERING THE STORM...The 2008 World Club Challenge was played in the teeth of a gale at Elland Road. Sinfield kicked three goals and a drop in Rhinos' 11-4 victory over Melbourne Storm.

though they won their final eight matches, Rhinos as a team and Sinfield individually went through some tough moments. A 68-0 drubbing of Celtic Crusaders in Newport took Rhinos into top spot, but only after farcical scenes in the build-up to the game.

Sinfield explained: "We stopped at a hotel in Bristol for a team meal, but there was a U2 concert on in Cardiff that night and the traffic was horrendous. We got stuck in a jam, some of the lads got changed on the coach and we arrived about 10 minutes before kick-off.

"It was like playing under-nines again, when it is all a rush and last-minute. We did a quick warm-up and then came out and blitzed them from the kick-off. We were 30-0 up after half an hour and I remember saying 'we should do this more often'."

Sinfield landed eight successful kicks that day, becoming only the second Leeds player, after Lewis Jones, to pass 1,000 goals for the club.

The following week Rhinos beat Saints 18-10 at Headingley to virtually seal top spot, but the captain suffered a fractured cheekbone, an injury which kept him out of the final round win at Salford City Reds which secured the league leaders' shield.

Rhinos' management kept the severity of the injury quiet and Sinfield returned in the opening round of the play-offs. "That was bitter-sweet," he recalled of the 44-8 victory at home to Hull KR. "It was good to pick up the result and get through the game okay, but Chev Walker suffered a badly broken leg, right in front of the South Stand.

"It was a nasty one, one of those that really sickens you. It is never nice seeing any player get injured, especially not a friend and former teammate. It just shows that some bad stuff can happen in rugby league games sometimes."

The 2009 season was the first in which the controversial club call system was used. That allowed the highest-ranked

TOUCHDOWN...Kevin Sinfield scored only 86 tries in his 521-game Rhinos career, so - like this one in 2008 - they were always worth celebrating.

84

WORRYING THE WARRIORS... Sinfield tests the Wigan defence during a 2008 encounter.

DOUBLE DELIGHT... Rhinos retained the championship in 2008 with another Grand Final conquering of St Helens, enabling Kevin Sinfield to lift the trophy for the third time. It was also Jamie Jones-Buchanan and Ryan Bailey's third triumph.

PRIZE GUYS... Kevin Sinfield kicked four goals in the 2008 Grand Final triumph and his kick also created a crucial touchdown for Danny McGuire, sparking raucous celebrations.

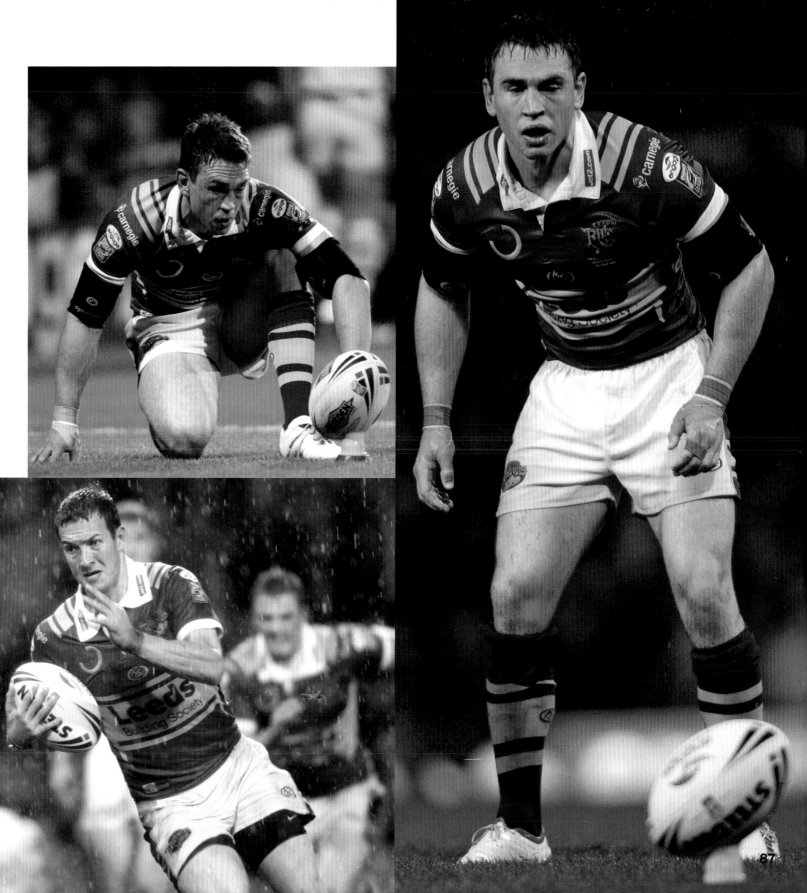

team after the first round of the play-offs to select their semi-final opponents.

Rhinos picked Catalans Dragons, who had finished eighth, to play at Headingley. Sinfield said: "Bluey was cool and calm about it; he told us all along he would pick the lowest-ranked team left in. It was the natural thing to do, but it probably did give Catalans some extra motivation.

"They had nothing to lose and everything to gain, but we got through it. It was an emotional win because John Holmes, who is one of the club's all-time greats, had died in the week before the game."

So Rhinos returned to Old Trafford to face St Helens for the third successive year. Once again, Leeds were determined to prove they were worthy champions against a team who felt they had been robbed of the title in previous seasons.

The game-breaker in Leeds' 18-10 win proved to be Lee Smith's try from a Danny McGuire kick late on. Saints felt Smith had been offside and Sinfield – who won the Harry Sunderland award as man of the match - said: "I can remember it being replayed and replayed before the video ref gave it.

"It was 50-50 and could have gone either way. Sometimes you need a bit of luck, but I would like to think our endeavour and the way we played that year made us worthy champions."

Though he was known as a motivator, Sinfield also paid tribute to McClennan's tactics, throughout the season and on Grand Final night.

"We watched footage of teams who had won three successive titles and the theme of 'three' was used a lot that year," Sinfield said. "It was 8-8 at half-time and I can remember Bluey saying he wanted a score in our first attacking set. I kicked a drop goal and that was a big psychological blow. It was smart tactics from Bluey."

Having accomplished the 'three-peat' Rhinos were hot favourites to win the title again in 2010, but it proved to be a disappointing

BLUEY...Brian McClennan's infectious enthusiasm brought the best out of Rhinos and inspired them to back-to-back Grand Final wins, as well as the league leaders' shield in 2009.

campaign which included painful defeats in two big games.

Rhinos were edged out 18-10 by Melbourne Storm in another World Club Challenge showdown at Elland Road and suffered a 30-6 drubbing by holders Warrington Wolves in the Challenge Cup final.

"The Melbourne game was a big disappointment," Sinfield conceded. "We lost and I had to come off with a dead leg. I missed the next four games and it was probably the most painful injury I have had. Even three weeks later I had to get up in the night to keep my leg moving; it throbbed all the time and I couldn't sleep, couldn't train and couldn't walk properly."

Back in the team, Sinfield helped Rhinos to fourth spot in the table and a first appearance at the new Wembley, but they were without two key players for the knockout final.

"We played Castleford away two weeks before Wembley and I was rested," he recalled. "I watched the game on TV and we lost JP with a knee injury and Luke Burgess, who had been playing really well, due to a fractured jaw.

"They were both a big loss. JP was unreal week in and week out. I knew how desperate he was to play for his hometown team at Wembley and we were always going to miss such a warrior in a game like that."

Sinfield, whose son Jack was team mascot, had no excuses for one of Leeds' poorest-ever performances in a final. He said: "We were fired up to do well, but emotion got the better of us. We trained well, the fans travelled down in numbers, but we just fell flat. We didn't perform."

Rhinos pulled off a shock win at league leaders Wigan Warriors in the play-offs, before the same team ended their hopes of a return to Old Trafford by inflicting a 26-6 defeat in the qualifying semi-final at Headingley. Danny McGuire suffered a knee injury in the first tie which ruled him out of the second and the early part of 2011.

Sinfield scored all Leeds' points in their final game of the year, taking his tally for the campaign to 262, but that proved to be the last time he would be coached by McClennan.

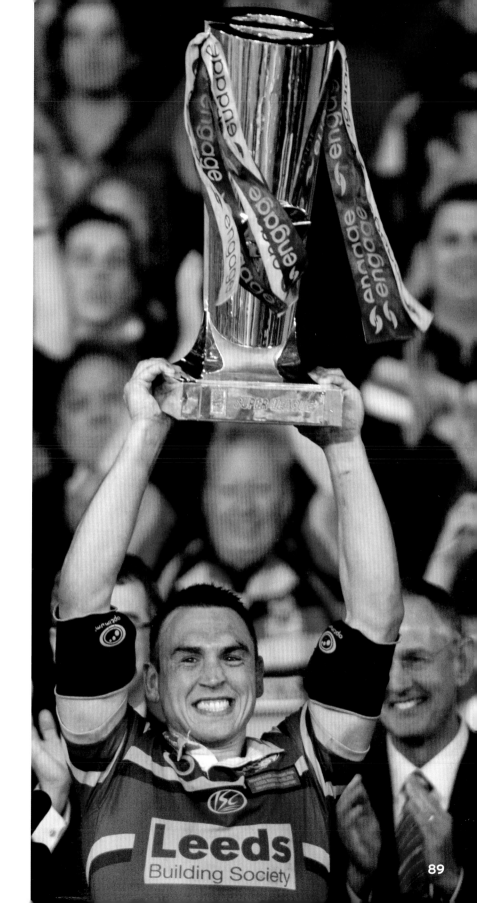

THREE-PEAT...Rhinos won an historic third successive Grand Final in 2009. St Helens were again the victims.

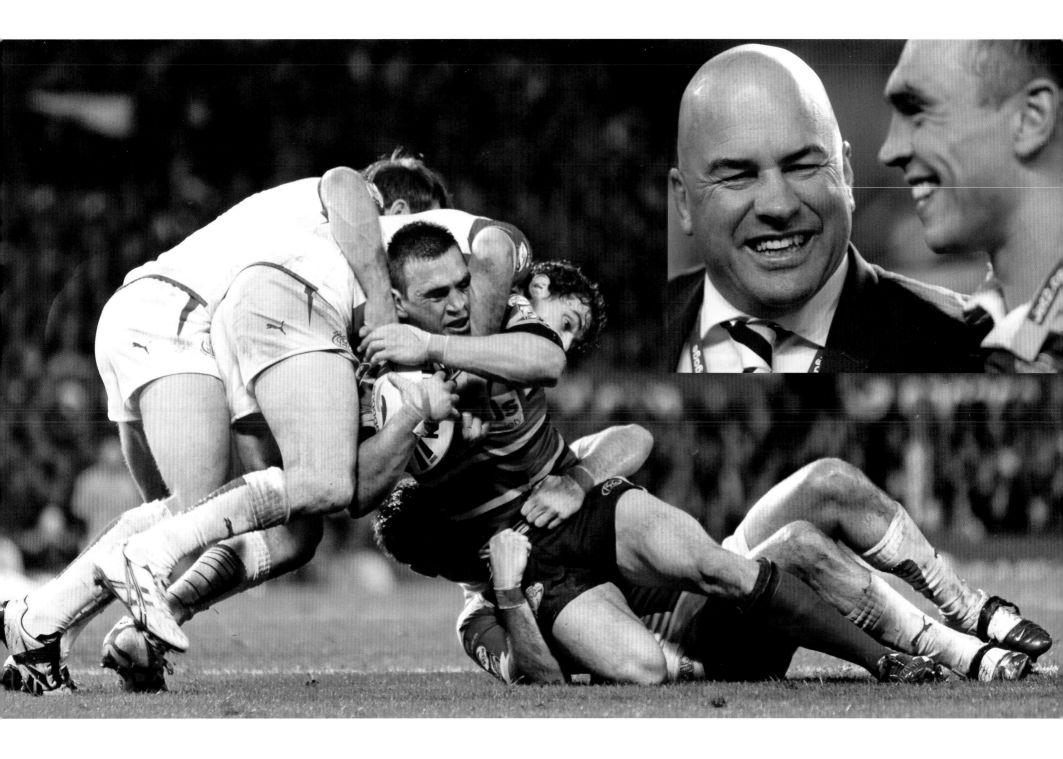

KEEPING COOL...The 2010 season began on a snow-covered pitch in Wrexham, where Rhinos froze out newcomers Crusaders.

YES SIR... Jamie Peacock and Kevin Sinfield receive a lecture from referee James Child in 2010.

BLOWN AWAY... Rhinos could not match Australian champions Melbourne Storm in the 2010 World Club Challenge at Elland Road.

SHATTERED DREAMS... Rhinos were well beaten by Warrington Wolves at Wembley in 2010. It was a tough blow for Carl Ablett, Keith Senior and Kevin Sinfield.

CHAPTER EIGHT
NEVER WRITE OFF A RHINO
2011-2012

Leeds Rhinos played two semi-finals during 2011 and in both of them Kevin Sinfield landed a last-gasp penalty to win the game.

The first was a Challenge Cup tie against neighbours Castleford Tigers at Keepmoat Stadium in Doncaster.

Tigers, the underdogs, were 8-2 ahead with seven minutes left, but Kallum Watkins touched down and Sinfield converted to level the scores.

Sinfield and Rangi Chase both failed to hit the target with a late drop goal attempt and the game went into sudden-death extra-time, with the first team to score going through to the final.

Two minutes into the third period Danny McGuire was tackled high by Castleford's Ryan McGoldrick and Sinfield kept his nerve to send Rhinos to Wembley for a second successive year.

Then, in a Super League qualifying semi-final, Sinfield attempted to break a 24-24 deadlock at Warrington Wolves with a drop kick two minutes from time. Richie Myler shot out of the defensive line to charge the kick down, touch judge James Child spotted he was offside and referee Steve Ganson awarded a penalty. Side-on to Warrington's most vociferous fans, Sinfield again brushed off intense pressure to send his kick between the uprights, securing a stunning

two-point win and a place in the title decider.

Those weren't isolated occasions. The skipper landed crucial goals throughout his career, including in a 2012 Super League semi-final, but how did he manage to keep his cool in such nerve-shredding situations?

"I've always been aware of what those kicks mean and the responsibility of taking kicks like that," Sinfield said. "If they go over you can come away as the hero, but I also understand you can end up being the villain. You just try and focus on it as another kick, no matter how important it is. You rely on technique, practice and preparation.

"Once the kick has gone over, relief is the main emotion. It is part of my job and I don't look on it as anything special, it is just about doing my job and carrying out my role in the team. Afterwards, on the bus or when you're at home, you start to think 'it's a good job that one went over'!"

Tellingly, Sinfield did not celebrate either kick. Explaining his muted reaction, he said: "I am quite respectful of the opposition. I know what it is like to lose in the last minute and in big, big games. You have to be aware of what the other team are going through."

The history-making 2011 and 2012 seasons were two of the most extraordinary in the Leeds club's history and were strikingly similar, with Rhinos crawling off the canvas on each occasion to upset the odds at Old Trafford.

In Sinfield's opinion, the catalyst for the Super League trophy's return to Headingley was the sudden appointment of Brian McDermott as coach in the autumn of 2010. The former Leeds assistant and Harlequins boss had originally been recruited as right-hand man to Brian McClennan, but stepped into the hot seat when the Kiwi, unexpectedly, quit.

"It was a surprise when Bluey left," Sinfield reflected. "He had done some wonderful things for us in the three years we had with him and he really freshened the place up, but bringing Brian McDermott in was a really shrewd move.

"He was absolutely brilliant for me as a player. He has got a real human touch about him, he is very, very honest and he is the best coach I have ever had. In so many areas he was excellent and I really enjoyed working under him."

McDermott took over without having had time to plan an off-season and Rhinos struggled badly for much of his debut campaign. By Easter they had played 10 Super League games and won only three, but Sinfield insisted that was due to the "quality of the competition" rather than anything Leeds' coach or players were doing.

"By that stage Super League had really levelled out," he said. "Leeds are expected to be in the top two all the time, but that is a bit disrespectful to the other teams. A lot more clubs were spending the full salary cap and that creates a level playing field. Recruitment had really stepped up and a lot more teams were creating their own players from their academies."

On July 10, 2011, Rhinos faced Catalans Dragons in Perpignan and were crushed 38-18. It was their third straight defeat and left them eighth in the table and in real danger of not qualifying for the play-offs, with only five games left.

"It was rock bottom," Sinfield said. "The result was the culmination of a lot of things that went wrong for us on the day; there were no excuses, we weren't good enough and I

think that was the stage when we said enough is enough.

"After every game you have a team meeting and go through a review and see what you can take from it. Catalans away was one when we thought 'we can't be this bad again'. It was a turning point for us, but at the time we were still very positive.

"I think other teams would have imploded and struggled to get it back, but Brian Mac's leadership during that tough period was outstanding and some of the senior players, the likes of Jonesy, JP, Kylie, Rob and Danny Mags, really stepped up.

"We stuck together and turned things around. You get great satisfaction when it all comes right, but sometimes you have to go through dark days first. Catalans away was certainly one of those times when everything that could go wrong, did."

The result turned the heat up on McDermott, but Sinfield recalled: "He never once transferred that to the players. He took the pressure off the lads and instilled confidence in the team. He really showed his leadership skills and he deserves a lot of credit for the way we finished the year."

Rhinos suffered just two more defeats after the Catalans debacle, winning 11 of their final 13 games. The second of those losses was against Wigan Warriors at Wembley, though Leeds put up a better than expected fight in a 28-18 scoreline.

"A couple of big decisions in the second half took the game away from us," Sinfield remembered. "But there were no excuses or complaints, the best team won on the day. I have never been one to blame referees and I am not going to start now.

"Wigan had a very good team that year; they played well and did a job on us. It was very disappointing, you come away from the ground feeling stripped, like you have been gutted from the inside, but coming through things like that hardens

YET AGAIN...Wigan inflicted Leeds' second Wembley defeat in as many seasons in 2011.

KNOCKOUT KINGS...Rhinos faced sudden-death throughout their 2011 play-offs campaign. Sinfield scored a crucial try in the opening win over Hull (left) and was outstanding as Warrington were stunned in the qualifying semi-final.

you. It gave us a steely determination to finish the year on a high."

Rhinos certainly did that. They climbed to fifth on the final league table, which earned them a home tie against Hull in the opening round of the play-offs, but meant they would be playing sudden-death rugby all the way through, while the top-four could afford to lose their opening match.

After seeing off Hull, Rhinos won at fourth-placed Huddersfield and were then chosen by Warrington Wolves, the league leaders, to travel to HJ Stadium in the qualifying semi-finals. The 26-24 victory that night was arguably the best in Leeds' history and certainly one of the club's most unexpected triumphs.

"We had a bit of momentum by then," Sinfield said. "All the pressure was on Warrington and after the season we'd had, we just decided to go there and enjoy it. But we weren't ready to finish just yet. It was a great team performance and we grabbed a fantastic win."

So Rhinos went on to face third-placed St Helens, yet again, in the Grand Final at Old Trafford. Rhinos led 8-2 at the break, went 16-8 behind, but came home with a wet sail in the fourth quarter to claim the trophy 32-16.

Substitute Rob Burrow was a unanimous winner of the Harry Sunderland man of the match award, scoring a sensational solo try and then setting up a brilliant touchdown for Ryan Hall. Sinfield said: "He was playing a bit of a different role then, coming on as hooker. But Rob is a fantastic professional; he is always willing to put the team first. He can score or create fantastic tries out of nothing, but to do it on the biggest

BEEP BEEP...Rob Burrow scored one of the great Grand Final tries in Rhinos' 2011 success against St Helens, to his teammates' delight.

HISTORY MAKERS...In 2011 Leeds became the first team to win the title from fifth on the table. It was a personal triumph for Sinfield and Brian McDermott, in his debut season as coach.

stage, like he did that night, showed what a quality player he is."

The following year was what Sinfield described as a "carbon copy" of McDermott's first season in charge, though it began on a real high when Rhinos beat Australian champions Manly Sea Eagles 26-12 in front of a World Club Challenge full house at Headingley.

Having become the first team to win the title from fifth in 2011, Rhinos were faced with having to do it again and for the second successive year, Grand Final glory followed Wembley heartbreak.

Warrington made it two wins in three seasons against Leeds at the national stadium with a 35-18 success in the Challenge Cup final, the fifth time Sinfield had captained a losing team in the knockout showpiece.

Tony Smith's men were so dominant that afternoon there seemed little prospect of Leeds overturning the odds if the teams met at Old Trafford, which in itself seemed unlikely given the opposition Rhinos would have to beat first.

"The play-offs were as difficult a run of games as we'd had all year,"

ZAK'S THE WAY TO DO IT...Zak Hardaker burst onto the Super League scene in 2011 and was a Grand Final try scorer.

WATCH THE BIRDIE...Kevin Sinfield met the real article as he promoted the 2012 World Club Challenge against Manly Sea Eagles. The pair didn't get on!

Sinfield said. "We played Wakefield first up at home, they had won eight on the bounce and that was a real test for us. At the start of that run I looked at the possible fixtures and Wakefield at home was the most difficult one, because they had no pressure on them.

"We won that and had to go to Catalans next, but having finished fifth the year before there was a real belief about us and the shackles were off, because nobody really expected us to do anything.

"We had a great win in France and I can remember Ryan Bailey making a break from a kick-off to set up a try for Magsy. That was a great moment for Bails and the team. We flew back straight after the game, which was the first time we had done that and it was a masterstroke, because it gave us more time to prepare for the semi-final."

Again Rhinos were the league leaders' club call pick. Wigan this time opted to face the champions, and came unstuck as Sinfield's last-gasp penalty secured a shock 13-12 victory, after the home side had led with two minutes remaining.

Wigan looked on course for Old Trafford when they overturned an 11-0 half-time deficit, but in the final moments Sinfield's bomb was spilled by full-back Jack Murphy, standing in for the injured Sam Tomkins. Rob Burrow cleverly ran at defender Liam Farrell, who was offside and Sinfield nailed the resulting kick.

Warrington, second in the league, faced Leeds for a second final in six weeks, but this time the tables were turned as

RED FACED: Rhinos dyed their hair for Comic Relief ahead of a trip to St Helens in 2012. The laugh was on them as they lost 46-6. (Dave Williams)

LOAN RANGER...Shaun Lunt was a key acquisition for Rhinos in 2012. His try saw off Salford in the Challenge Cup fifth round.

Rhinos retained the trophy with a magnificent 26-18 victory, despite going behind to an early Richie Myler try.

"It was a brilliant night," Sinfield said. "To turn it around from the Cup final, play like we did and beat them was unbelievable and very, very special."

The Leeds captain scored his team's opening try and booted five goals from as many attempts. Remarkably, he did not miss with a single kick in the entire play-offs campaign. His final tally for the season was a club record 173 goals, five more than Iestyn Harris had managed in 1999.

Both 2011 and 2012 were a tale of Leeds getting up after being knocked down. That was literally true of Sinfield in Leeds' second successive Grand Final triumph. With the

game in the balance early in the second half he was clattered by Warrington's Michael Monaghan following an attacking kick near Wolves' line. There were worrying scenes as Leeds' medical team rushed on, but the stand-off regained his feet, shook himself down and played on.

"I was knocked out," Sinfield confirmed. "But the game meant so much to me I did not want to come off. Fortunately, I came round pretty quickly and I was desperate to stay on and be part of us winning the game."

Under current rules Sinfield would have had to leave the field for a concussion assessment, but that law was yet to be introduced. He conceded: "Looking back, it wasn't the smartest thing I have ever done, but there were no ill-effects. Rhinos' medical staff are fantastic and if they had any doubts

TACKLED...Sinfield is brought to ground in unconventional fashion against Salford in 2012.

Opposite: ZAK'S FANTASTIC...Zak Hardaker is mobbed by Jamie Jones-Buchanan, Danny McGuire and Kevin Sinfield after scoring in Leeds' 2012 Challenge Cup semi-final win over Wigan.

LE CRUNCH... Rhinos recorded an amazing win at Catalans Dragons en-route to the 2012 Grand Final. Ben Jones-Bishop makes a break in that game.

they would not have let me play on.

"I was monitored for the next few minutes and I was okay. Getting the Harry Sunderland was the icing on the cake and I felt really good about the game and the part I played in it, but it was a really good team performance."

Sinfield looks back at the time between the agony of Wembley and ecstasy at the Theatre of Dreams as possibly the finest spell of his entire Leeds career.

"I played some of my best rugby in those six weeks and it was a really enjoyable time," he reflected. "We had such a tough run, but we stuck together and came through it and to turn around the result from the Cup final was fantastic. I

think Warrington felt we had snatched it away from them the year before and they were going to put that right, but we owed them after Wembley and to overturn that and win the trophy from fifth spot again was absolutely unreal."

The Harry Sunderland award wasn't the last honour Sinfield received in 2012. At the end of the year he collected the Golden Boot, presented by Rugby League World magazine to the planet's top player.

Sinfield was a controversial choice among Australian pundits, who could not accept an Englishman being the world's best. He said: "When you play a team sport it is always difficult to accept individual awards, but it was very nice to be rewarded with something like that. The award was for the team though, I just did my job to the best of my ability and I was fortunate to get recognised for it."

Of the Australians' reaction, he went on: "I was aware of it, but it didn't bother me. It is all about opinions and people always see things differently. I didn't put myself up for it and I didn't have a vote, I was just pleased somebody thought I was doing things right."

SIMPLY THE BEST...Kevin Sinfield with the Golden Boot trophy he won in 2012.

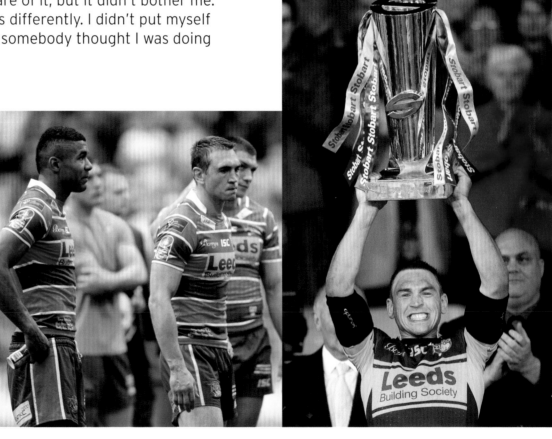

AGONY TO ECSTASY...A third successive Wembley defeat was followed in 2012 by a second straight Grand Final triumph. Warrington Wolves were the opposition in both games.

GOLDEN BOOT...Sinfield came out on top against another legend, Adrian Morley, at Old Trafford in 2012. He battled through the pain barrier to get his hands on the trophy for the sixth time.

JOY OF SIX...The 2012 Grand Final victory was the sixth title win for Kevin Sinfield, Jamie Jones-Buchanan and Ryan Bailey.

CHAPTER NINE
DREAMS DO COME TRUE
2013-2015

After 15 years of trying and six losing finals, Leeds Rhinos finally got their hands back on the Challenge Cup in 2014. For Kevin Sinfield, who had collected five runners-up medals – all as captain - the walk up the steps to receive the trophy from Castleford legend and former Leeds coach Malcolm Reilly was the end of a very long road.

Rhinos' run of three successive appearances in the final ended in 2013 when they were knocked out at the fifth round stage by Huddersfield Giants. Rhinos, who started the year with a hard-fought 18-14 loss to Melbourne Storm in the World Club Challenge at Headingley, finished third in Super League and got as far as the final round of the play-offs, but ended the year without having appeared in a major domestic final for the first time since 2006.

Despite their six Grand Final victories, Rhinos went into 2014 with only one Challenge Cup winner in their squad, Jamie Peacock having been a member of the Bradford teams which beat Leeds in the 2000 and 2003 deciders.

Pressure from the media mounted on Leeds every time a new Challenge Cup competition came around and at 33, Sinfield knew time was running out to complete his collection of every available honour in the club game.

"Actually our Challenge Cup record was very good," Sinfield said. "We had probably won as many Cup ties as anybody else, but we just couldn't win the big one. The media had created a monkey on our backs, but we tried to play it down as a team."

Sinfield struggled to put his finger on exactly why Rhinos, so good in Grand Finals, could not get it right when it really mattered in the Challenge Cup. He admitted: "My mindset was a bit different towards the Challenge Cup, for some reason. It has always been to pick myself up and go again if I get knocked down, but after the third, fourth and fifth losses in Challenge Cup finals I found it really hard to do that. I was going to keep having a go at it, but I was beginning to think it might not happen, that we wouldn't be good enough to get it. That was something I was prepared to live with."

The feeling ahead of the 2014 campaign was that while the current generation of players was the greatest in the club's history, they would not be remembered as true legends if the team broke up without having collected the famous silver trophy.

The road to Wembley in 2014 began for Leeds with a 60-6 romp at Wakefield Trinity Wildcats, when Sinfield kicked eight goals. He booted six more when they saw off St Helens in the fifth round, despite losing Rob Burrow to a serious shoulder injury, but ironically the toughest game in Leeds' entire run was the quarter-final, at home to Championship outfit Leigh Centurions.

The visitors pushed Rhinos all the way before Leeds edged

SUPERMEN...Super League teams wore special superhero kits for one of the 2013 rounds. Sinfield and Wigan's Sam Tomkins were ideal models. (Mark Robinson/© Sky Sports)

SOUPER MAN...Being captain leads to some unusual tasks. Kevin Sinfield promotes Super League's latest sponsor on a cold day in 2013.

through 25-12. The fact Sinfield kicked a drop goal, along with four two-pointers, illustrates how tight it was. Warrington were hot favourites in the semi-final at St Helens, but Rhinos produced their most impressive performance of the season to battle into their fourth final in five years, 24-16.

Daryl Powell, who had appointed Sinfield as Leeds captain 12 years earlier, was in the opposing corner at Wembley after guiding Castleford Tigers to their first Cup showpiece since 1992, when Sinfield had featured in the curtain-raiser to their defeat by Wigan. Powell's men had some outstanding league form under their belt, but Leeds travelled to Wembley as favourites. For once, the all-West Yorkshire decider went as the bookies expected, Rhinos breaking their hoodoo with a convincing 23-10 victory in which man of the match Ryan Hall bagged a brace of tries and Sinfield kicked three goals.

There were memorable celebrations on the pitch and in the Leeds end of Wembley when the final whistle blew, but reflecting on the long-overdue triumph Sinfield said: "Was it worth the wait, worth losing five finals for? I'd say not. I enjoyed it and it was great to get my hands on the trophy, but I'd much rather have won it a lot earlier. Overall I was just grateful to get my hands on the Cup and be part of a winning Wembley final."

There was one other new experience for Sinfield in 2014 and it also came in a game against Castleford. A month before the final Sinfield was sent-off for the only time in his rugby league career, for butting Tigers' Luke Dorn during a Super League derby at Headingley.

Explaining what happened, Sinfield said: "Nobody believes me, but I didn't mean to headbutt him. It was like animals in the wild locking horns when they are in battle or being aggressive to each other; we were having verbals, I thought we were both going to lean in and put our heads together, but he pulled away and I went through with it!

"People want to think for a split second I lost it, but it wasn't like that at all. It was an accident as much as anything."

WRONG FOOTED...Sinfield and Chris Clarkson isolate Melbourne Storm's Cooper Cronk during the 2013 World Club Challenge.

DERBY DRAMA...Sinfield had some epic tussles with Castleford Tigers during his Rhinos career. This game was in 2013.

TOUCHDOWN...Kevin Sinfield evades Joel Monaghan to score for Rhinos in a play-off tie at Warrington in 2013. Leeds lost 40-20.

WALK OF SHAME...Kevin Sinfield was sent-off just once in his career, against Castleford in 2014. Jamie Jones-Buchanan and Zak Hardaker offer their condolences.

Sinfield admitted the incident came out of frustration at a series of incidents in the match. He recalled: "At the start of the game Justin Carney knocked me for six and I hurt my knee. I had to have surgery to get it sorted out in the off-season. Late on we were winning by six and in front of their posts. I was screaming at Paulie Aiton to give me the ball, to drop a goal so we'd win the game, but he didn't hear me, it went to Danny Mags and then Carl Ablett knocked-on off his backside.

"Dorn picked up and made a break and I went in for the tackle. He was holding me down and kicking out, trying to milk a penalty and he kicked me on my bad knee and then in the nuts. So in the space of about five seconds I'd gone from a chance of winning the game, to having to make a tackle to

stop a break, being penalised and kicked in the knee and the nuts. I got up and I was angry, but I didn't mean to headbutt him. If he hadn't pulled out I don't think anything would have come of it."

Down to 12 men, Rhinos could not hold out and Tigers hit back to salvage a 24-24 draw. Sinfield was banned for two games and his first match back was the Cup semi-final against Warrington.

"It isn't something I am proud of, but I don't regret it," Sinfield said of the red card brandished by referee Ben Thaler. "It was another experience. I have experienced most things in the game and that was something new. You always learn from any new experience and it probably worked in our

FINALLY...Jamie Peacock, Kylie Leuluai, Kallum Watkins, Zak Hardaker, Ryan Hall and Carl Ablett all contributed to Leeds' first win at the new Wembley.

CUP KINGS AT LAST...Rhinos won the Challenge Cup in 2014, ending 15 years of hurt. Ryan Hall produced a man of the match performance during Sinfield's first victory after five losses in finals. Jamie Peacock and the skipper were equally jubilant afterwards.

SIXTH TIME LUCKY...After five previous defeats, a loss to Castleford in 2014 would have been unbearable for Sinfield and his long-suffering teammates. There was no doubting how much it meant once the final whistle sounded.

HOME OF HEROES...The Challenge Cup and cricket's county championship were both brought home to Headingley in 2014. Yorkshire's captain was Andrew Gale.

FALL GUY...Sinfield is upended against old foes Warrington Wolves in 2014.

ON YOUR BIKE...Rhinos wore a one-off yellow kit against Catalans Dragons in 2014, to celebrate the Tour de France visiting Leeds.

SURE FOOTED...Sinfield rarely put a foot wrong in 2015 after returning to the side following a spell on the sidelines.

ON THE CHARGE...Sinfield gives Hull KR's defence the slip during his final season.

favour when the Cup semi and final came around. It gave me a couple of weeks off to rest my sore knee and I went into those games feeling fresh and with even more motivation."

With the final piece of the jigsaw, the Challenge Cup, in place, Sinfield began to ponder his long-term future and the possibility of scratching a persistent itch. Having never played a game of rugby union in his life, a new challenge in the 15-a-side code was something which had always appealed.

"When I had surgery on my knee in the off-season it gave me chance to reflect on my career and where I wanted to go next," he said. "In about December I started to think seriously about playing rugby union. Being realistic I would only have played on until the end of 2016 with the Rhinos.

"I had always wanted to have a go at union, but kept putting it off. When you talk to young kids you tell them about chasing their dreams and having no regrets. I decided to do something for myself; I didn't want to retire from playing and have any 'what ifs'."

On March 31, 2015, Sinfield stunned a packed press conference, as well as rugby league fans all over the world, by announcing he was to join Rhinos' sister club Yorkshire Carnegie at the end of the year. The aim, he said, was to play his final game of rugby league at Old Trafford.

"It was a good opportunity for me," he insisted. "I wanted to stay in Leeds and I thought I would get a good chance of some game time with Carnegie, rather than going to a Premiership club who might not know what to do with me. I'd

ACE MARKSMAN...This became a familiar sight for Leeds Rhinos fans during Kevin Sinfield's 19-year career.

have had to uproot my family and as a 35-year-old who was new to the sport I might have ended up sitting on the bench for most of the time."

Jamie Peacock had already confirmed he would be retiring at the end of 2015 so a fairytale script was being written, though the dream ending at that stage seemed unlikely. Rhinos had finished sixth the previous season, which was their poorest Super League performance since the competition's debut year of 1996. They lost all their four games after Wembley and exited the play-offs at home to Catalans Dragons in the first round, so were not rated as genuine contenders for honours, particularly after making just one off-season signing.

Opposite: SUITED, NOT BOOTED...Kevin Sinfield, dressed to impress.

As it turned out, Australian forward Adam Cuthbertson proved to be an inspired recruit and went on to be nominated for the Man of Steel award, which was won by teammate Zak Hardaker.

Rhinos were never out of the top-four and led the table at the time of Sinfield's announcement, but even so the long-serving captain admitted he didn't think a trophy treble was likely. He said: "I always wanted my final game to be at Old Trafford, helping Rhinos win the Grand Final.

"As the other two trophies got closer and closer, thoughts of the treble began to come to the fore. But the reality is it was my 19th season, so I'd had 18 previous attempts to win the treble and not managed it, or even come close, so it was going to be very, very tough."

BENCHED...Kevin Sinfield was left out of the side for a spell in 2015. The other Rhinos player is young hooker Robbie Ward.

The Challenge Cup was retained in August with a record-breaking 50-0 rout of hapless Hull KR at Wembley, where Sinfield kicked seven goals and Tom Briscoe ran in five tries. Jamie Jones-Buchanan did not play in the final after being injured in the last-four win over St Helens, but was involved in one of the day's most memorable images when he and Sinfield lifted the Cup together.

The 2015 season was an agonising one for the long-serving forward, who was limited to just 11 appearances. He returned in time to feature against Saints at Warrington, but his bad luck resurfaced when he suffered serious damage to a quad muscle late in the tie.

Sinfield recalled: "I really felt for him. We played so well and we were jubilant in the changing rooms afterwards, but at the same time I was devastated for Jonesy. I went to see him and he was lying on the physio's couch in the doctor's room. He was dejected and completely disheartened; there was no way I could make it right, but I felt the best way I could help was by saying we wanted to win the Cup for him and if we did, would he lift it with me? That brought a smile to his face.

"I think over the next few weeks he forgot about that, but I didn't. When the final whistle went at Wembley we embraced and I said to him 'Are you ready to lift it with me?' He was quite reluctant, but I think he understood why I wanted him to do it; he has contributed so much to the team and the club and been a fantastic help to me.

"It didn't make up for him not playing, but I think it was a nice thing to do and it showed what a great squad we had and how much people cared for each other. I hope it's something Jonesy and his family will never forget."

By the time of the Cup triumph, at the end of August, the captain was re-established in the team after being dropped to the bench and then out of the side altogether for a spell earlier in the season.

Sinfield only cemented his spot back in the side when

500 NOT OUT...Kevin Sinfield made his 500th appearance for Rhinos in 2015, but was on the losing side to Warrington Wolves at Headingley.

Inset: TWO LEGENDS...Kevin Sinfield receives a memento to mark his 500th Leeds game from the only other surviving player to achieve the feat, John Atkinson. Sinfield's 521 appearances have been bettered only by John Holmes (625) and Fred Webster (543). Atkinson played 518 games.

youngster Liam Sutcliffe suffered a season-ending knee injury and he conceded: "It was tough. It was the first time I'd been left out for a long time and you never forget it when it happens to you. But I am not naïve enough to think I am too good or too big a player to be left out.

"There was a lot of competition in my position and it was another time when I had to get up, fight back and try and regain my place. I don't look back on it now as a horrendous time; it was just one of those disappointments you have to deal with. It is a test and you have to show character, but we all got what we wanted in the end."

It threatened to be a case of déjà vu after Wembley as Rhinos, who had led the table by six points at one stage, suffered three successive defeats. The third of those was at home to Castleford, after Sinfield suffered a severe dead leg and had to hobble off in the first half.

A new system was introduced in 2015. Super League split into two after 23 matches, with the top-eight battling for the title and bottom-four fighting against the Championship's leading quartet to retain their elite status.

After a further seven league games the top-four on the Super League table went into knockout semi-finals for a place at Old Trafford: First versus fourth and second at home to third. So Rhinos needed to finish in the top-two

to secure a home tie in the play-offs and that was beginning to look unlikely. Sinfield recalled: "I remember sitting in the dugout as the Castleford game unfolded. It looked like we wouldn't finish top, because Wigan would go above us if they beat Saints the following night, so I might have played my last game at Headingley as a Rhino.

"It was a desperately disappointing time, but then Saints did us a favour by beating Wigan with a very late try and, unexpectedly, we went into the final round still top of the table. I didn't watch the Saints-Wigan game, but after it I got a load of very positive text messages from players, coaches and staff saying 'we're still in this'.

"Our last game was away at Huddersfield and we could finish anywhere from first to fourth. That week I was hobbling around and was only about 70 per cent fit, but I had a jog the day before the match and decided to give it a go. The rest is history."

Sinfield duly started at stand-off in possibly the most incredible game Super League has ever seen. Losing 16-8 with seven minutes remaining, Rhinos were set to finish third and return to Huddersfield - who would bag second spot - for the following week's semi-final.

Wigan were winning at home to Castleford and therefore seemed on course for the league leaders' shield. The RFL had hired a helicopter to take the trophy to either Wigan or Huddersfield and it set off from Barton airfield, in Salford, for DW Stadium when Leeds slipped eight points behind.

But then Tom Briscoe scored in the right-hand corner and Sinfield landed an astonishing conversion, under huge pressure, to cut the gap to a single goal. The significance of that kick tended to be lost in what was to follow, but had he not nailed the conversion, the treble would never have happened.

GIANT KILLER...Rhinos finished top of the table in 2015 by beating Huddersfield Giants in their final league game. Sinfield defied injury to play and landed an equalising penalty, before Ryan Hall's last-gasp try sealed victory.

IT'S RYAN HALL...As the hooter sounded to end the final game of the season, Leeds' winger dashed over for a try to seal top spot on the table. (1. Dave Williams)

With less than two minutes on the clock Giants conceded a penalty just to the right of the posts and the captain opted to take the two, rather than kick to touch in an attempt to score a winning try. Rhinos were settling for a draw and home advantage against Huddersfield the following week, but there was one more twist to come. Sinfield landed the kick and Giants restarted with one minute left to play. With five seconds remaining Danny McGuire chipped through, Ryan Hall picked up, swerved past Giants' full-back and suddenly found himself with a clear run to the line as the hooter sounded. The try was awarded after a check with the video referee and Leeds had won the game and league leaders' shield. The helicopter, within sight of Wigan's ground, was rerouted to Huddersfield.

"I've never experienced anything like it," Sinfield said. "I've never won a game with a try on the last play before,

definitely not one that important - and one that meant a helicopter carrying the trophy had to be turned around in mid-air.

"It was unbelievable. Leeds' support has always been fantastic, at home and away, but the Rhinos' end was full that night and celebrating in front of our own fans while we waited for the trophy to arrive - and then lifting it with JP - was very, very special. It is something I will never forget."

Wigan finished second and demolished a demoralised Huddersfield, who were third, in the first semi-final.

Rhinos again seemed down and out when they trailed by five points late in the following week's semi-final against Saints, but Sinfield - showing all his experience and leadership skills - landed a 40-20 kick to turn the game on its head. Leeds scored a try in the resulting set and went on to win 20-13, setting up an Old Trafford showdown with Wigan.

So Sinfield, Peacock and Leuluai got their wish of bowing out at Old Trafford and the dream came true in spectacular fashion as Rhinos, yet again, dragged themselves off the canvas. Leading 16-6 at the break they went 20-16 behind in the third quarter, only for rookie forward Josh Walters to score an equalising try.

Walters had joined Rhinos the previous year from Yorkshire Carnegie. Sinfield, about to make the opposite move, converted and Leeds held on to win 22-20, so the captain's

1,792nd goal for Rhinos was what secured an historic treble, the first time the club had won every available trophy.

"I could not have finished in a better way," Sinfield said. "I was just very, very grateful to do it with that team and as part of the best club in the world. It was fantastic and I was very, very fortunate. Everyone who plays sport has a way they would like to finish and only a very, very small percentage get to go out the way they would like to. But I was just part of the team; I was thankful to the club, the rest of the players, the coaches and the fans for making a dream come true."

BRAINS TRUST...Rhinos' 2015 coach Brian McDermott and chief executive Gary Hetherington.

LEAGUE LEADERS...Rhinos celebrate finishing top of the table. The shield was delivered to Huddersfield by helicopter.

SURPRISE HERO...Josh Walters was a shock selection for the 2015 Grand Final, but scored Leeds' crucial try.

GOLDEN GOAL...This was Kevin Sinfield's final place kick for Rhinos. It edged them to victory over Wigan Warriors in the 2015 Grand Final and secured an historic treble.

THE PERFECT ENDING...Rhinos completed the treble by beating Wigan 22-20 in the 2015 Grand Final. Sinfield's final points for the club made the difference. It was a fairytale finale for Jamie Peacock, Sinfield and Kylie Leuluai in their last game.

WINNERS ARE GRINNERS...Josh Walters holds the trophy his try helped secure, flanked by Brett Delaney and Brad Singleton. Departing trio Jamie Peacock, Kevin Sinfield and Kylie Leuluai enjoyed the celebrations, as did wingers Tom Briscoe and Ryan Hall.

FAMILY MAN...This picture with sons Sam and Jack and wife Jayne was taken in the stand at Old Trafford by Kevin's dad Ray soon after the end of his last game, the 2015 Grand Final.

VICTORY SONG...Danny McGuire leads the team chant in the Old Trafford changing rooms after Rhinos' 2015 title success.

FAMILIAR SIGHT...But this was probably the sweetest, as Sinfield shows off the Grand Final trophy for the seventh time, in 2015.

133

CHAPTER TEN

SIGNIFICANT OTHERS - THE CLASS OF 2015

In what is probably a unique achievement for rugby league, the Leeds Rhinos squad which won every available trophy in 2015 contained two members of the British Empire. Jamie Peacock was awarded an MBE in the 2012 New Year Honours and two years later Sinfield found his name on the Queen's birthday list.

"We'd been at Center Parcs for the weekend and when we got home the official letter was waiting," Sinfield remembered. "At first I thought it was from the Inland Revenue! When I opened it, it was a huge surprise.

"It didn't say I had been awarded an MBE, it just asked if I would accept one. I quickly filled it in and sent it back, but I didn't know if I would actually be getting one. There was a lot in the letter about secrecy, so I couldn't tell anybody. I told my parents and my wife Jayne, but I didn't want to mention it to anyone else in case it turned out I wasn't going to get one after all. Fortunately it went through and I was humbled and honoured to be recognised for services to rugby league."

That is a theme which runs through all the awards Sinfield has collected during his career, including when he was runner-up in the BBC's Sports Personality of the Year voting at Christmas, 2015. Sinfield was the first rugby league player to be nominated for one of the most prestigious prizes in British sport and he might have won it but for the Great Britain tennis squad's triumph in the Davis Cup the weekend

the shortlist was confirmed.

Andy Murray was hurriedly added to the nominations and he topped the poll for the second time in three years, with 361,446 votes. Sinfield stunned the BBC by coming second on 278,353. World champion athlete Jessica Ennis-Hill received 78,898 votes in third place.

Second place has never been good enough for Sinfield, but in this particular case it was a triumph for the former Leeds captain and the thousands of supporters, from across rugby league, who put club allegiances aside and joined forces to vote for him. He said: "I was so, so grateful to every single person who voted for me. I can't thank them enough."

Simply having a player nominated was a step forward for rugby league, which is usually given a meagre few seconds' airtime during the Sports Personality broadcast. Sinfield added: "I was just delighted to be among the 12 nominations. Everything else was a bonus."

The awards ceremony was held in Belfast and Rhinos' treble-winning team joined him on stage when he was interviewed before voting began. "I was really nervous," he revealed. "My hands were freezing cold and sweating at the same time. It wasn't because I was up for the award, but I knew I was representing rugby league and the Rhinos and I didn't want to mess it up.

"It was great to be the first rugby league player nominated and I saw it as a chance to show people who don't know our sport that we are good people. I wanted to leave a positive impression, not for me, but for everybody who plays, watches and cares about the game.

"It is tough when you play a team sport, because you are dependent on others. I was nominated alongside individuals who had won world titles, but I couldn't have achieved anything in 2015, or throughout my career, without the team around me. They all deserved it as much as I did and I was really glad all the boys were at the event."

Niall Carson/PA/Press Association Images)

Kevin Sinfield has fond memories of most of the players he turned out alongside during his long career, but Leeds' all-conquering 2015 squad developed a special bond. Here is his assessment of the players who made history.

Zak Hardaker

Full-back.
Man of Steel.
31 games, 13 tries, 9 goals, 1 drop goal.

"An unbelievable talent and a worthy Man of Steel in 2015. He has got every attribute you want in a rugby league player and was instrumental in our success. He has got a fantastic amount of skill and was a pleasure to play alongside. He will only get better."

Tom Briscoe

Winger.
Lance Todd Trophy winner.
17 games, 15 tries.

"Possibly the most naturally strong back I have ever played alongside – his hips and backside are unbelievably powerful. Opposing teams struggle with getting him to ground, his quality shines in big games and he was one of the main reasons we got on the front foot. He is a lovely bloke as well."

Kallum Watkins

Centre.
Player of the year.
32 games, 20 tries.

"The best British centre by a mile, one of the top three or four in the world and you'll see the best of him in the next five or six years. If you wanted to construct a rugby league player you would build Kal. He is a fantastic athlete; he has got skill and pace and great feet. I loved playing on the right side with him and Tom."

Joel Moon

Centre.
32 games, 15 tries.

"In a word, class. He has got so many different skills and could play in most positions on the field. He is great to have around the team and the squad and was my regular breakfast buddy. He seems to glide when he runs and I don't remember ever seeing him have a bad game."

Ryan Hall

Winger.
31 games, 22 tries.

"Just seems to get better and better. He is vastly experienced and I think he will take a leadership role over the next few years. Strong and a great finisher, he has a habit of grabbing important tries that nobody else could have scored."

Danny McGuire

Half-back.
Harry Sunderland award winner.
33 games, 17 tries.

"A pleasure to play alongside and one of our best players in 2015. Magsy, Zak and Adam Cuthbertson could all have been named Man of Steel and would have deserved it. His game has changed over the years, but he has always been top-class. I've roomed with him quite a few times and he is a great mate."

Rob Burrow

Half-back/hooker.
30 games, 12 tries.

"Like Magsy, I played alongside Rob for a long time and enjoyed every minute. The three of us combined very well and we enjoyed so many good moments in so many big games. Rob has had to adapt his game, coming off the bench and playing hooker as well as scrum-half, but he always puts the team first. He's a top, top player with a unique skill-set."

Kylie Leuluai

Prop.
22 games, 2 tries.

"He was a big help to me, especially in the tough times. Another lovely bloke and as tough as they come; a real smiling assassin. He put his body on the line in 2015, when he was playing with a heart condition and I was delighted he got the rewards he deserved."

Paul Aiton

Hooker.
27 games, 3 tries.

"I was really sad to see Paulie go, when he signed for Catalans Dragons. It was desperately disappointing he got injured and missed the two finals in 2015, but a fantastic person to play alongside and somebody who would have become a massive fans' favourite."

Jamie Peacock

Prop.
34 games, 3 tries.

"An absolute warrior, I played alongside him for 10 years and we became great mates. A lot of times in 2015 he would hobble into training and it would look like he had no chance for the weekend, but then he would put his boots on and have a stormer. He is one of the all-time greats, not just at Leeds, but in rugby league."

Jamie Jones-Buchanan

Back-row.
11 games, 0 tries.

"My best mate in the game, we played for England Schoolboys and came through the academy together and have been teammates ever since. I owe him so much; he is not only a great friend, but also an inspiration every day. He has a positive attitude towards everything and is the most competitive person I have ever met."

Carl Ablett

Second-row.
36 games, 12 tries.

"Underrated, but a fantastic player. Will go down as one of the most durable and versatile players in the group, having won Grand Finals at centre and in the back-row. He was our only ever-present in 2015 and I think he is another one who will really step up into a leadership role over the next few years."

Stevie Ward

Back-row.
28 games, 5 tries.

"I was delighted when he was handed the No 13 shirt after me. He had a fantastic year in 2015 and would have played for England, I am sure, if he hadn't been injured in our final league game. He has a hard-running style and the skills of a half-back, is already very experienced in his early 20s and has the attributes of a future captain."

Brett Delaney

Back-row.
26 games, 4 tries.

"Frogger is an unsung hero. He is a grafter who does all the messy stuff nobody else wants to. He puts his head in where it hurts, which means he has problems with injuries at times, but always delivers in big games."

Mitch Achurch

Back-row.
20 games, 3 tries.

"He has had unbelievably bad luck with injuries, but has great skill for a big man. I was delighted for him when he got to play in the 2015 Challenge Cup final and pick up a winner's medal."

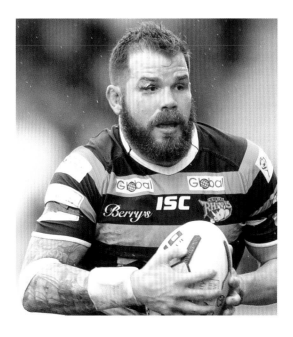

Adam Cuthbertson

Prop.
Man of Steel nominee.
34 games, 9 tries.

"I wish I was younger, so I could have played alongside Cuthbo for longer. One of the best overseas signings the club made in my time. He had an unbelievable first year and he is a stand-off playing in a front-rower's body. We forged a great relationship in a short space of time. He's a top bloke."

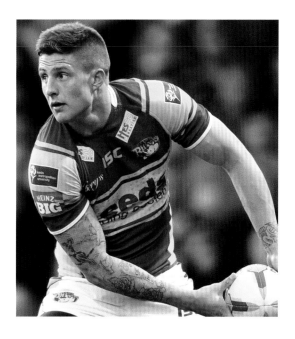

Liam Sutcliffe

Stand-off.
15 games, 6 tries, 25 goals.

"Sutty will be a big part of the club's future. He has got a lot of experience already at a young age and has the skill and athleticism to go all the way in the game. I have spent a lot of time with him and been really impressed with his character. He is a top player who will become a legend at the club."

Brad Singleton

Prop.
34 games, 9 tries.

"He had to be patient, but made a breakthrough in 2015. Playing in both finals – and winning – was the confidence booster he needed. He's a good bloke to have around and has a big future in the game."

Jimmy Keinhorst

Centre/second-row.
17 games, 6 tries.

"I was devastated for him when he was left out of the Cup final in 2015, but how he bounced back says a lot about him. He is a great team player, the way he switched from centre to back-row was awesome and he is another one who has a big contribution to make over the next few years."

Josh Walters

Second-row.
Old Trafford try scorer.
11 games, 2 tries.

"I am a big fan. Coming from rugby union to league he has acquitted himself really well and scoring the important try at Old Trafford will have done him the world of good. Never moans, just gets on with his job and always gives his all."

Andy Yates

Prop.
10 games, 1 try.

"If you need a penalty, send Andy on. Teams seem to like to knock his head off. He only played a handful of games, but never let anybody down. It was a shame he had to move to Wakefield to progress his career, but I wish him all the best."

Robbie Ward

Hooker.
3 games, 0 tries.

"Desperately unlucky not to play more games than he did. He is very talented and will be back in Super League before long."

Rob Mulhern

Prop.
2 games, 0 tries.

"Only played twice in 2015, but was around the squad all year and made a big contribution in training. He is a good bloke and I think JP's influence at his new club Hull KR will take him to the next level."

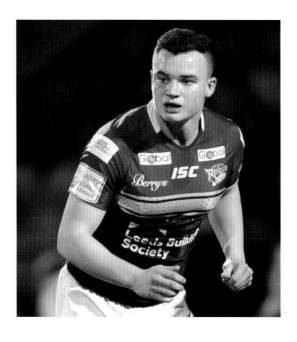

Ashton Golding

Full-back.
4 games, 0 tries.

"One for the future. He had a long spell out with a serious back injury, but overcame that and showed up well when he got a chance. He has a touch of class about him."

Ash Handley

Winger.
20 games, 13 tries.

"Got his chance when Tom Briscoe was injured and took it with both hands. He would be a regular starter at any other Super League club."

Jordan Lilley

Half-back.
4 games, 1 goal.

"Somebody I have a lot of time for. He made his debut in 2015 and showed up really well, even when he was playing at hooker rather than half-back. Jordan is another star of the future."

Mitch Garbutt

Prop.
14 games, 1 try.

"What a signing he was. He wasn't in the team at Brisbane, came to England and won three trophies in 14 games. He is another top bloke who settled in really well and totally committed himself to the cause."

What those players produce on a Friday night or Sunday afternoon is the product of a huge amount of effort from a group of unsung heroes. According to Sinfield, Rhinos could not have achieved their success without the efforts of what he believes is the leading backroom team in the game.

"It's no secret I rate Brian McDermott as the best coach I've played under," Sinfield said. "His leadership has been tremendous, especially in the tough times and in 2015 he was right at the top of his game.

"He is very thorough and the hours he puts in are frightening, but he gets results. He works really well with his assistants, Barry Eaton and Chris Plume. They deserve a lot of credit. They tend to do a lot of the field work and Mac oversees it all. What they deliver as a coaching team is second to none and has been at the heart of our success over the last few years."

Sinfield believes McDermott's appointment was a masterstroke by chief executive Gary Hetherington, who is somebody else the ex-skipper has a high regard for. He said: "Gary and the chairman Paul Caddick have

Brian McDermott

Coach.

transformed the club since they took over in 1996. It was on its knees then and look at how things are now.

"Gary is very, very shrewd and he has made some outstanding decisions. Signing Adam Cuthbertson and Mitch Garbutt were good examples of that. He works really well with Rob Oates and Chris Gibson.

"Rob is Mr Leeds Rhinos; he's the best commercial director in the sport, but he also lives and breathes the club and his enthusiasm is infectious. Chris is a link between the players and the club, he used to play for Leeds in the 1970s and he understands the team's point of view, but he can also see the other side of things. He is a great mentor, supporter and friend. He has been like the glue that binds it all together."

The conditioners and medical staff are also vital to the operation. Sinfield added: "Jason Davidson and Chris Black did a fantastic job. It is tough when you have got a squad of 25-30 and you have to deliver a program that caters for all their individual needs, but somehow they managed it. Being able to provide a bespoke program for the entire group was a brilliant feat. Jason is also our unofficial team manager and fixer, sorting things like hotels for away games and making sure we are where we need to be at the right time. Chris does a lot of work with the boys who aren't playing, he keeps them in great shape and he is a reason why somebody like Josh Walters can step straight in and make an impact."

Rhinos' medical team is headed by Dr Jon Power and physiotherapist Andy Barker, assisted by Dr Paul Lanfear and physio Ben Harper plus masseurs Steve Clegg and James Collinge. Sinfield said: "They are all great people, who know a lot about their job. It's not just physical fitness, they have a counselling role as well and if anything does go wrong it is brilliant

Barry Eaton
Assistant coach.

Chris Plume
Assistant coach.

Gary Hetherington
Chief executive.

Chris Black
Conditioner.

Dr Jon Power
Club doctor.

Andy Barker
Head physio.

James Collinge
Masseur.

James Bletsoe
Analyst.

Glynn Bell
Kitman.

Rob Oates
Commercial director.

Chris Gibson
Mentor.

Jason Davidson
Head of athletic performance.

Dr Paul Lanfear
Club doctor.

Ben Harper
Assistant physio.

Steve Clegg
Masseur.

Ryan Golding
Head groundsman.

Phil Daly
Media manager.

Billy Watts
Time keeper and club legend.

to know you have got people of that quality behind you."

Sinfield picked out five others whose contribution to the cause largely goes unnoticed. He said: "Our head of analysis James Bletsoe does all the stats and puts together videos for the coaches and the motivational stuff. He is very, very thorough and does a terrific job.

"Glynn Bell, the kitman, has a touch of obsessive compulsive disorder about him, but that's a good thing because it means he makes sure everything is spot on. He has to ensure everything's ready for us when we get to the ground and every i is dotted and t crossed. Having someone as efficient as him around makes a big difference.

"Ryan Golding and his grounds staff are outstanding and do a fantastic job producing a quality pitch and training facilities all year round.

"Phil Daly is the best media manager in the game, very efficient and intelligent.

"The final cog is Billy Watts, who has been at the club even longer than I was. He was timekeeper, helper and a sort of unofficial good luck charm. He had a tough year personally in 2015, but he was always smiling, always cheerful and a lovely bloke to have around. He has retired now and will be sorely missed."

2000

2001

2004

2005

2008

2009

2012 Leeds Building Society

2013 Leeds Building Society

STATS

KEVIN SINFIELD'S RUGBY LEAGUE CAREER

LEEDS RHINOS (1997-2015)

1997
2 substitute appearances

1998
2 substitute appearances, 1 try, 4 points

1999
9 starts (12 sub), 2 tries, 12 goals, 32 points

2000
19 starts (7 sub), 7 tries, 28 points

2001
32 starts (1 sub), 10 tries, 29 goals, 1 drop goal, 99 points

2002
30 starts, (2 sub), 8 tries, 32 goals, 96 points

2003
34 starts (1 sub), 6 tries, 122 goals, 5 drop goals, 273 points

2004
31 starts, 4 tries, 152 goals, 3 drop goals, 323 points

2005
31 starts, 6 tries, 149 goals, 2 drop goals, 324 points

2006
26 starts, 3 tries, 105 goals, 1 drop goal, 223 points

2007
32 starts, 6 tries, 139 goals, 3 drop goals, 305 points

2008
34 starts, 4 tries, 137 goals, 3 drop goals, 293 points

2009
29 starts, 4 tries, 121 goals, 3 drop goals, 261 points

2010
29 starts, 4 tries, 121 goals, 4 drop goals, 262 points

2011
36 starts, 2 tries, 160 goals, 2 drop goals, 330 points

2012
37 starts, 7 tries, 168 goals, 5 drop goals, 369 points

2013
28 starts, 4 tries, 106 goals, 2 drop goals, 230 points

2014
27 starts, 5 tries, 102 goals, 2 drop goals, 226 points

2015
26 starts (4 sub), 3 tries, 137 goals, 3 drop goals, 289 points

Leeds Rhinos total
521 appearances (490 starts + 31 as substitute), 86 tries, 1,792 goals, 39 drop goals, 3,967 points

GREAT BRITAIN (2001-2003, 2005, 2007)

8 starts (7 sub), 2 tries, 18 goals, 44 points

ENGLAND (2000-2001, 2008-2013)

26 starts (3 sub), 5 tries, 100 goals, 220 points

LANCASHIRE (2001-2003)

3 starts (1 sub)

CAREER TOTAL

569 appearances (531 starts + 38 sub),

93 tries, 1,910 goals,

39 drop goals,

4,231 points

HONOURS:

Grand Final winner x 7

Grand Final runner-up

Challenge Cup winner x 2

Challenge Cup runner-up x 5

World Club Challenge winner x 3

World Club Challenge runner-up x 3

League leaders' shield winner x 3

Leeds Rhinos and Super League records for most goals and points

Super League record for most appearances

Third most appearances for Leeds

Third-highest rugby league points scorer

England's highest points scorer

2005 World Club Challenge man of the match

2005 Lance Todd Trophy winner

2009 and 2012 Harry Sunderland award winner

2012 Golden Boot

2015 Sports Personality of the Year runner-up.

FANS OF KEVIN SINFIELD

Emma-Jayne Abbey
Angela Abbott
James Abbott
Kathleen Abbott
Mark Abbott
Phil Abrahamson
Tracey Acaster
Tommy Ackroyd
Ian Adams
Craig Adcock
George Adcock
Graham Adkin
David Ainley
Christopher P. Ainslie
Alfie Alderson
Rosie & Steve Alderton
Andy & Kirsten Aldridge
Dave Allen
Gareth Allen
Richard Allen
Gerry Alleyn
Sami Allison
Richard Douglas Alton
Richard James Alton
Lis Ambrose
Brian and Anne Amos
David Amos
Keith Anderson
Paul Anderson
Simon Anderson
Michael Andrews
Sara Andrews
Alan Anslow
David Anthony
Patrick Stephen Anthony
James Appleby
Mike Archenhold
Anthony Archer
Rich Archer
Adam Armitage
Donna Armitage
Lynnette Armitage
Maureen Armitage
Michaela Armitage
Mick Armitage
Neville Armitage
Trevor & Jackie Armitage
David Arnold
Elizabeth Arnold
Peter Arro
Neil Arundel
Andrew Ashby
David and Caroline Ashmore
Jon Ashton
Peter Ashworth
Keith Askin
Allan Aspinall
Craig Asquith
Dana Asquith
David Asquith
Jenny Atkinson

John M Atkinson
Louise Atkinson
Phil Atkinson
Robert Atkinson
Sam Atkinson
Susan Atkinson
Mandy Atter
Hazel Ault
Jason Paul Avison
William Babbington
Jim Backhouse
Simon Backhouse
Ted Bacon
David Bailey
Jayde Bailey
Jo Bailey
Peter Bailey
Robin Bailey
Dave Bainbridge
Raj Bains
Leslie Baker
Lewis Baker
Mark Baker
Robert Baker
Denise Balaban-Smith
Georgina Baldwin
Jamie Balint-Dewhurst
Claire Ball
Patrick Ball
Sue Ball
Chris Balmforth
Jennifer Ann Bampton
Walter A Bampton
Jennie Band
Ed Banks
Graham Banks
Jonathan Banks
Oliver Banks
Paul Banks
Joel Barber-Nicholson
Maisie Barber Nicholson
David Roy Barker
Graham Barker
Mick Barker
Neil Barker
Rachael Barker
Rachel Barker
Dave Barnes
Graham Barnes
Philip Barnes
Tricia Barnes
Aaron Barraclough
Michelle Barraclough
Mick Barraclough
Sharon Barraclough
Clare Barran
Richard Barrett
Sue Barrett
David Barron
Kerrie Barrow
Katie Bartle

Stephen Bartlett
Troy Bartlett
Linda Barton
Alan Bass
David Bass
Nicholas Bass-Woodcock
Karl Bates
Tristan Bates
Richard Batley
Sarah Batters
Danny Battle
Paul Baxter
John Bean
Ken and Christine Beanland
Mark Beardow
Heather Beaumont
Andrew Beck
John Beckett
Robert Bedard
Tony Bedard
Stephen Bedford
Jade Beecroft
Trevor Beeton
Andrew Belcher
Philip Belgardt
Daniel Bell
Francess Bell
Michael A Bell
Brian Bellhouse
Brian Bellwood
Sian Belt
Alison Bennett
Darren Bennett
David Bennett
Lynn Bennett
Jessica Bentley
Claire Berry
Roy Berwick
Tony Bettison
Michael & Brenda Bettison
Garry Bickerdike
John Bickers
Les Billingham
Anita Bilton
Kathryn Bingley
Marcus Bingley
Barry Binns
Joe Binns
Paul Binns
Jamie Birdsall
Martin Birkin
Ethan James John Biscombe
Dave Blackburn
David Blackburn
Terry Blackburn
Andrew Blacker
Barry Blackshaw
Robert Blackwood
Hannah Blagg
Elliot Dale Blair
Annamarie Blakey

Eric Blakey
Nick Blane
Ray Blay
Debbie Bloomfield
David Blythe
Tom Blythe
Paul Boldy
William Bolton
Chris Boneham
Keith Boneham
Sean Booth
Andy Booth
Anne Booth
Chris Booth
David Booth
Duncan Booth
Mark Booth
Matthew Booth
Milton Booth
Susan Booth
Stephen Boothroyd
Anne Bosanquet
Terry Bossons
Jayne, Nigel & Faye Bottomley
Christopher Bowden
Ken Bowe
Eric Bowen
Michael Bower
Jason Bowers
Bob Bowman
Jessica Bowman
Andrea Boyd
Tim Boyes
Harry Boynton
Andrea Bracewell
Bradders
Chris Bradley
Liam Bradley
Stuart Bradley
Charlie Brady
Gill Braithwaite
Andrew Bramley
Simon Brasnett
Denise Bray
Mandy Brearley
Alex Bremer
Stephen Brennan
Adrian Brett
Julie Brewer
Steph Brewis
Jane Brice
Andrew Brierley
Louise Kate Brierley
Jordan Briggs
Harry Brigham
Richard Brightwell
Strachan James Brittain
Noel Britton
Bernard Britton
Scott Broadbent
Chris Broadbent

Derek Broadbent
Jason Broadbent
Ross Broadfield
Reg Broadhead
The Broadhurst Family
Kevin Brock
Geoff Brocklehurst
Matthew Brocksom
Simon Brocksom
Vicky Brocksom
James Brook
John Brook
Wayne Brook
Anne Booth
Ernie Brooks
Nicholas Brooks
Ethan Brooksbank
Mathew James Brotherton
Andy Broughton
Alan Brown
Craig Brown
Lawrence Brown
Robert Brown
Ron Brown
Sandra Brown
Scott Brown
Eddie Browne
Paul Broxholme
Janet Bryant
Matthew Bryant
Jacquie Bryars
Mike Bryars
John Buckley
Marc Buckley
Richard J Buckley
Stephen J Buckley
Kyle Buckley-Mayall
Dan Budby
Kevin Budden
The Bull family
Julie Bullock
Martin Bullock
Paul Bullock
Hannah Louise Bulmer
Craig Bunko
Tracy Bunko
Ronald Burden
Alex Burdon
Roy Burdon
Yasmin Burdon
James Burgan
Debbie Burgess-Gough
Charlotte Burhouse
Stuart Burnell
Chris Burns
John Burns
Christian Burrill
James Burrill
Tony Busfield
Paul Bussey
Angela Butler
Bryan Butler

Glyn Butler
Sheila Butler
Ian Butterfield
Rick Butterfield
Tracey Butterfield
Steve Butterworth
Jon Bygate
David Byrne
John Bywell
Joe Cable
Philip Cable
David Caddick
Brendan Cafferty
Lesley Cain
Luke Cain
Colin Caine
Jonathan Caine
Jamie Cairns
Liz Cairns
Derek Calpin
Angie Calvert
David Calvert
John Calvert
Mark Calvert
Richard Calvert
Al & Jacqui Cameron
Ann Campbell
Stephen Campbell
Donna & Peter Cariss
Nicholas Carling
Catherine Carlton
Stephen Carlton
David Carncross
Chris Carnegie
Jane Carnegie
Martin Carr
Michael Carr
Stephen Carr
Terry Carr
Michael Carrier
Brenda Carter
Lewis Carter
Andrew Cartlidge
Sally Cartmell
Anne & David Cartwright
Darren Carty
Daniel Cassidy
Dave Catterick
Charlotte Causey
Jonathan Causey
Andrew Cavadino
Andrew Cave
John Cawthorne
Steve Cawthorne
Ethan Claire Stephen Chadwick
Marie Chadwick
Matt Chambers
Stephen Chambers
Andrew Chapman
Anna Leigh Chaplin
Chris Chapman

David Chapman
Jim Chapman
Kevin Chapman
Ned and Cynthia Chapman
Adam Chapman-Smith
Brenda Chappell
Robert E Chapple
Nathan Charles
Trudy Charlton
Gracie Chatten
Jackie Chatten
Alan Cheadle
Kirsty Cheetham
John Chew
Richard Chew
Nick Chidlow
Norman Child
Allison Chin
Clover Chinner
Keith Chisem
Alexander Carl Christie
Jacob Chutter
Henry Clappison
Graham Claridge
Mrs A Clark
Ben Clark
George Clark
Helen Clark
James David Clark
Matty Clark
Stuart & James Clark
Michael J Clarke
Robert Clarke
Stuart Clarke
Mandy Clarkson
Tom Clay
Joseph Clayson
Darren R Clayton
Master Zack Clayton
Martyn Cleaver
Stuart Cleaver
Mark Clegg
Nick Clegg
Stan Cleghorn
Andrew Clough
Jackie Clowes
Neil Coates
Zoe Cockburn
Steve Cocking
Kirsty Coggill
Mark Cohen
Tony Cohen
Andrew Coldrick
Brian Coleman
Jarrad Collins
Jo Collinson
Stephen Collinson
Blake Colton
John Connaughton
Martin Conneely
Chris Connolly

Chris Connor
Tony Cook
The Cook Family
Michael Cooke
Andrew Richard Cooper
Garry Cooper
Gill Cooper
Pauline Cooper
Robert Cooper
Steven Cooper
Wendy Cooper
Lucy Cope
Georgia Copley
Susan Copping
Bob Corbett
Ian Corfield
Helen Coser
Danny Cothay
Steve Cottrell
Paul Coull
James Matthew Coulson
Lee Coupland
Christine Cowling
Zac Cowlishaw
Andrew Cox
Anthony Cox
Charlotte Cox
Dominic Cox
Fiona Cox
Gregory Cox
Maggie Cox
Susan Cox
Tim Cox
Paul Craggs
Charlotte Cranage
Josh Cranage
Robert Glenn Crann
Dave Craven
Geoffrey Craven
Phil Craven
The Craven Family
Beau Oliver Creasy
Andrew Crombleholme
Andy Crompton
Kenneth Crompton
Rob Cromwell
Kevin Crookson
Dawn Crosby
June & David Crosland
Josh Cross
Luke Crossfield
Martin Crossling
Marjorie Edith Crosswaite
Tom Crouch
Wendy Croy
Terry Cubiss
Nigel Cuddy
Mark Cull
Brendan Cunningham
Geoffrey Cunningham
Joanne Cunningham
Joseph Cunningham
Kath Currie
Ciaran Curtis
Damian Curtis
Sid Cussons
Mark Cusworth
Martin Cusworth

Keith Dabill
Brian Dalby
Michael Dalby
Thomas Iain Dale
Jennifer Dales
Abi Daly
Michael Daly
Sandra Daly
Danny Dance
Alan Daniel
Ewan Daniel
Paul Darbyshire
Phil Darley
Nikki Darling
Claire Darlow
Miriam Darlow
Mike Davenport
Joseph Davey
John E. Davidson
Alun Davies
Fiona Davies
Joe Davies
Mick Davies
Stephen Davies
Steve Davies
Thomas Davies
Caroline Davis
George Davis
Helen Davis
Simon Davis
Val Davis
Colin Davison
Eric Davison
Terence Davison
Andrew Dawes
Rod Dawes
Shaun Day
Clare Dean
Glynn Dean
Stacie Dean
John Dearden
Gary Dearlove
Stuart Deaton
James Deaves
Lorraine Degraff
Andrew Deighton
John Dempsey
Andy Dennis
Deborah Dennison
Elliot Devaney
Malcolm Devereux
Chris Devine
Steve Dews
Paul Dibb
Steve Dickens
Kayley Dickinson
Mark Dickinson
Paul Dickinson
Samantha Dickinson
Sylvia Dickinson
Jack Dingley
Chris Dinsdale
Andrew Dixon
Harry Dixon
Josh Dixon
Katie Dixon
Mike Dixon
Nicola Dixon

Sue Dixon
Teresa Dmoch
Craig Dobbs
Chris Dobson
David Dobson
Jamie Dobson
Janet Dobson
Liz Dobson
Stephen Dobson
Malcolm G Dodd
Mark Dodd
Peter Doherty
Sean Donnelly
Paul Douglass
Carol Dove
Martin Dowling
Dave Downes
Paul Downes
Alex Dowse
Brian Dowson
Christopher Doyle
Diane Lois Doyle
Richard Drake
Stephen Drake
Dan Driver
Dennis Drury
Tom Drury
Nathan Drye
Daniel Duce
Carl Duckels
Paul Duckels
Andrew Dufton
Les Dufton
Janet Duncan
Gary Dunham
Joseph Dunham
Richard Dunn
Karen Dunne
Darren Dunnill
Darran Dunwell
Leejay Durrans
Jake Duxbury
David J Dyer
Gary Dyson
Irene Dyson
Dean Eagleton
Mark Eagleton
Ashley Earnshaw
Olivia Easby
Mark Eastham
Claire Easton
George Easton
Jim Eccles
Rachel Eden
Jack Edgcumbe
William Edson
David Edson
Andy Edwards
Michael Eglin
John Elliott
Catherine Ellis
David Ellis
Jack Ellis
Matt Ellis
Michael Ellis
Wayne Ellis
Bethany Ellwood
Chris Elsworth

Jonathan Emery
Ronster Emery
Mike Emmett
Enid Emms
James England
Sally England
Alan Etheridge
John Etty
David Evans
Peter Evans
Ryan Evans
Stephen Evans
Stephen Everall
Michael Eyres
Norman Fairbairn
Louanne Fairholme
Bowman Family
Martin Farley
Andy Farmery
Michael Farnell
Paul Farnell
Lianne Farr
Megan Farrell
Ben Fawcett
Jon Fawcett
Michael Fenton
Janette Fermoyle
Judith Ferris
Alistair Field
Jean Field
Kevin Field
Lee Field
Mark Fielder
Thomas Fincher
Andrew Firn
Colin Firth
Dale A Firth
John Firth
Margaret Firth
Sally and Peter Firth
Lucy Fisher
Sally and Dave Fisher
Joseph P Fitzgerald
Gordon Fitzgerald, Former
England RL Team Driver
Helen Fitzpatrick
Fitzy
Geoffrey Flaherty
Ian Flatres
Donna Flaxman
Claire Fleming
Steve Fleming
Thomas Fleming
Robert Fletcher
Stephen Fletcher
Hannah Ford
Patricia Forde
Steve Forde
Andrew Fornsworth
Susan Forster
Paul Forth
Danny Foster
Jack and Betty Foster
Peter Foster
Steve Foster
Maisie Fowell
Robert Fowkes
Matt Fowler

David Fox
Russell Fox
Sam Fox
Lauren Fozzard
Peter Frain
Daniel Frank
Steve, Keiran & Robbie
Frankland
Dave Franklin
James Franklin
Archie Franks
Mark Frearson
David John Freeman
Nick Fresson
Joe Frobisher
Ronnie Furie
Paul Gabriel
Julie Gaffigan
Jack Galbraith
Andrew Gale
Richard Gallagher
Danielle Gant
Freddie Gape
Craig Gardner
Marie Garner
Paul Garner
Philip R Garnett
Ken Garrett
Mary Garth
Jade Megan Gatiss
Damian Gaughan
Martyn Gaunt
Philip Gaunt
Saun Gaunt
Alan Gawthorpe
Jack Gawthorpe
Neil Gawthorpe
Callum Gay
Natasha Gay
Tracy Geary
Hazel Gee
Denis Gibson
Donald L Gibson
Rachel Gibson
Steven Gibson
Julia Gilbert
Karen Gilderdale
Ben Giles
Mark Gilham
John Gill
Mary Gill
Richard Gill
Sarah Gill
Simon Gill
Eileen Gisburn
Daniel Gittos
Jimmy Glaister
Kath Gledhill
Mathew Gledhill
Robert Gleeson
Ian Glover
Stuart Glover
Robbie Goddard
Lisa Godfrey
Max Wynzar Golding
Tom D. Goldsworthy
John Goldthorpe
Matt Gomersall

Arnold Goodfield
John Goodrick
Jonathan Goodrick
Michael Goodson
Glenn Goodwill
Will Gordon
George K Gough
Matt Gough
Ian David Gourlay
Margaret Gourlay
Howard Grady
Jonathan Graham
Leslie Graham
Malcolm Graham
Rosemary Graham
Steven Graham
Peter Grainger
Chris Grant
Mark Grant
Claire Grattan
Brian Gray
Daniel Gray
Liam Gray
P A Gray
Rob Gray
Katie Grayson
Stan Grayson
Mick Greaves
Gareth Greaves-Milner
Adam Green
Christopher Green
Vanessa Green
Wolfe Green
Keith Greenall
Helen Greener
Steven Greenhalgh
Nicholas Greenhalgh
Richard Greenhalgh
Colin and Sandy Greenwood
Eric Greenwood
Ruth Greenwood
Steven Greenwood
Gemma Greenwood-Field
Angela Gregory
Caoimhe Gregory
Eric Gregory
Michael Gregson
Sally Gresham
Kelly Griffin Wigan
The Groundwell Family
David Groves
Emily Gudgeon
Jon Guntrip
John Hackett
Peter Haddington
Billy Hague
Elizabeth Haigh
Kevin Haigh
Roy Haigh
Emma Hainsworth
Gary Hainsworth
Alex Hall
Angie Hall
Barbara Hall
David Hall
Dianne Hall
Emma Hall
Kathleen Hall
Michael Hall

Richard Hall
Susan Hall
Mark Hallam
Chris Hallas
Elaine Haller
Louise Haller
Chris Halliley
Neil & Ben Halliwell
Laura Halstead
Stephen Hambleton
Cathy Hamer
Alan Hammond
Ellie Hammond
Damien Hampshaw
Beverley Hampshaw
Peter Hampshaw
Philip Hampshaw
Raymond Hampshaw
Dean Hanahoe
Stephen Hanlon
Roy Hanna
Graham Hannah
Kersha Hannan
Adam Hanson
Ian Hanson
Karen Hanson
Alex Hardaker
Oliver Hardaker
Shauna Hardaker
Kristian Hardcastle
John Harding
Jason Hardwick
Neil Hardy
Jo Hardy and Phil Hardy
Gill Hargreaves
Anthony Harker
Ben Harker
Ema Harker
Sarah Harker
Aubrey Harris
Brian Harris
David Harris
Dean Harris
Mark & Jane Harris
Mark Harris
Matthew Harris
Sid Harris
Adam, Simone, Ben & James
Harrison
Annie Harrison
Ben Harrison
David Harrison
John Harrison
Sarah Harrison
David Harsley
George Hart
Tim Hart
June Hartley
Lynne Hartley
Kay Hartley
Kevin Hartley
Steve Haswell
Tony Hatton
Hazel Hawkes
Grace Hawkesworth m
Gareth Hawkhead
Jaci Hawkins
Diane Hawley

Michael Hawley
Tom Haworth
Karen Hayes
Malcolm & Glynis Hayes
Mark Haythorne
Craig Hazell
Graham Head
Geoffrey Heald
Jeff Heard
Norman Heath
Joe Heaton
Adam Hebbron
Madeleine Hegarty
Keith Helm
Brenda Henderson
David Henderson
Duncan Henderson
Jonathan Henderson
Richard Henderson
Sam Henderson
Steph Henderson
Terry Hepworth
Richard Hern
Melvin Herring
Jean Hesp
Neil Hester
Paul Hester
Kath Hetherington
Adam Hewitt
Anthony Hewitt
Christopher Hewitt
Richard Hewitt
Tom Hewitt
Joseph Hickey
Jack Hicks
Paul Hicks
Andrew Higgins
Nathan Higgins
Stephen Hiley
Dave Hill
David Hill
Graham Hill
John Hill
Richard Hill
Clifford Hillary
Jack Hinchcliffe
John Hinchcliffe
Paul Hinchcliffe
Lucy Hindle
Michael Hird
Stuart Hird
Alison Hirst
Joe Hirst
Harold Hirst
Tim Hiscoe
Richard Hoban
Owen Hobart
Carl Hobson
Richard Hodges
Mike Hodgetts
Steve Hodgetts
Brian Hodgson
Dave Hodgson
John Hodgson
Marjory Hodgson
Nikki Hodgson
Russell Hodgson
Steven Hodgson

Karen Hogg
Steve Holdway
Anthony James Hollings
Martin & John Holm
Christopher Holmes
Julie Holmes
Luke Holmes
Michael Holmes
Mike Holmes
Nigel Holmes
Denise Holroyd
Gillian Holroyd
John Holt
Karen Holt
Michael John Holt
Paula Holt
Richard Holtham
Irvin Homan
Julie Hooker
Beverley Hoole
Joel Hopkins
Carl Horigan
Mary Horn
Steven Horne
Nigel Hornegould
Tim Horner
Linda Horsey
David Horsfall
Matthew Horsley
Rob Hoskin
Stephen Houseman
Charly Howard
Keith Howard
Tim Howard
Joanne Howieson
Graham Howland
Beverley Hoyle
Amanda Huck
Andrew Huddleston
Daniel Hudson
Leon Hudson
Phil Hudson
Tony Huff
Dylan Hughes
Lee G J Hughes
Wendy Hughes
Charlotte Hull
Michael Hulme
Anthony Humpston
Kevan Hunt
Harry Hunter
Kevin Hunter
John and Glyn Huntington
Mark Hurd
Raymond Hurrell
David Husband
Gary Hutchinson
John Hutchinson
Phil Hutchinson
Trevor Hutchinson
Niel Hutton
Declan Hyland
Steve Ibbotson
Mark Ibitson
Robert Illingworth
Trevor Ingham
Beccie, Keith & Louise Ions
Victoria Iredale

David & Ann Jack
Maria Jackiw
Catherine (Polly) Jackson
Donald Jackson
Geoff Jackson
HarryJames Jackson
Josh Jackson
Linda Jackson
Matthew Jackson
Phil Jackson
Scarlet Jackson
Sheena Jackson
Michael David Victor Jagger
Michele Jagger
Tom Jagger
Lorraine Janiczek
Kingsley Jarrett
Janis Jarvis
Howard Jefferies
Sallie Jefferies & Rob Bedford
Terry, Sally, Mark and Luke Jeffery
Ken Jenkins
Sue Jenkins
Tony Jenkins
Matthew Jennings
Chris Jephson
Peter & Joan Bottomley
Amy Job
Andrew Johnson
Joseph Johnson
Irene Johnson
Paul Johnson
Stephen Johnson
Steve Johnson
Jenny Johnstone
Len Johnstone
Helen Jolly
Alan Jones
Anne Jones
Dawn Jones
Diane Jones
Mark Jones
Nathan Jones
Paul Jones
Steven Jones
Andrew Jordan
Sandra Jordan
Geoffrey Joseph
Chris Jowett
Daniel Andrew Jowitt
Colin Joyce
John Joyce
Gail Jubb
John & Andrea Jubb
Wayne Jubb
Nick Juden
Peter Judson
Neil Kaiper-Holmes
Gemma Kay
Carolyn Keenan
Chris Kelly
Edward Kelly
Phillip Kelly
Zoë Kempa
Patricia Kempton
Martyn Kenna
Alastair Kennedy

Hayley Kenny
Mark Kent
Paul Kent
Mick Kenworthy
Michael Keough
Arron Kerfoot
Cheryl Kershaw
Lynne Kershaw
Nadine Kershaw
Wendy Kettlewell
Anastasia Khrileva
Matthew Kidd
David Kilgannon
Lee Kilgannon
Ian Kilgannon
Jay Kilgannon
Mick Kilgannon
Amanda Kilgour
Bernadetta Kimmitt
Darren King
Jennifer King
Darrel Kingan
Andrew Kingston
Jim Kinsella R.I.P.
Allan Kirby
Amy Kirk
Jess Kirk
Jonathan Kirk
Nathan Kirk
Stephen Kirk
Christine Kirkbride
Kris Kirkbride
Samuel Kirwin
Amanda Kitchiner
Andy Kitching
Gareth Kitching
Gavin Kitching
Louise Kitching
Michael Kitching
Shaun Kitching
Andy Kitson
Bev Knaggs
Andrew Knight
Joshua Knight
Tom Knight
Brenden Knowles
Margaret Horton Koku
Chris Lamb
Pam Lamb
Trevor Lamb
Wilson Lamont
Frederick Land
Bethanie Lane
Paul Lanfear
Stuart Langdale
Peter Langley
Victoria Langley
Carl Langton
Dave Large
Family Latham
Guy Laughton
Barbara Lavelli
Mark Law
Jonathan Lawes
Richard Lawes
Peter Lawrance
Gillian Lawrence
Mikes Lawrence

Thomas Lawrence
Andrea Lawson
Matt Lawson
David Lawton
Keith Laycock
Pauline Laycock
Mike Lazenby (In Memoriam)
Rachel Lazenby
Simon Lazenby
Mike Leach
Rob Leadley
Brian Leaf
Greg Learoyd
Tom Learoyd
Arran Ledger
Daryl Karl Ledger
Jodie Lee
Richard Lee
Chris Leech
Nigel Leech
Michael Leeming
Bill Lees
Miss Pat Lees
Alex Lewis
David Lewis
Simon Lewis
Sue Lewis
Shannon Light
Tarnia Light
Victoria Light
Chloe Liley
Richard Lillie
Diane Lillywhite
Limon Loiners Pro Rege et Lege
Philip Lines
Tommy Liney
Clare Linklater
Amy Linley
Sue Linstead
Nick Lister
Paul Lister
Martin Little
Steven Llewellyn
William Lloyd
Emma Lockwood
Keith Lockwood
Paul and Brenda Lockwood
Alex Lodge
Ian Lofthouse
Samantha Long
Bryan Longbottom
Stuart Longbottom
Olivia Longthorpe
Michael Longthorpe
Colin Lonsdale
David Lonsdale
Jamie Lonsdale.
Sheldon Lord
Julie Lorriman
Laura Lounds
Paul Lowrey
David Lowther
Dave Lucas
Josh Lucas
Steven Ludbrook
Michael Lumley
Richard Lumley
Kevin Lunn

Mark Lunn
Richard James Lunn
Steve Lunn
Anthony Lupton
Michael Alan Lyall
Christopher Denis Lyons
Scott Lyons
Tony Lyons
Trevor Mabbitt
Michael Mabbitt-Granahan
Samuel Mabbitt-Granahan
Mall Machin
Dave Mackay
David Mackay
Mackie
Sophie MacNay
Maureen Patricia Madden
Lee Maddison
Wendy Maddison
Alan Madeley
Darran Madeley
Craig Maher
Carl Mahoney
John Peter Maitland
David Makin
Dannii Mallinson
John Mallinson
Sylvia Maltby
Andrew Manby
Sue Manby
Jo Maney
Peter Mann
Sam Manson
Andrew Marchant
Alan J Mark
Tracy Marran
John Marriott
Karen Marsden
Kewell Marsden
Kath Marsh
Sarah Marsh
Alastair Marshall
Ashley Marshall
Carl Marshall
John Marshall
Geoffrey Marshall
Lisa Marshall
Robert Marshall
Marshall Marshall Worsnop
Clare Martin
Gary Mason
Matthew Mason
Samantha Mason
William Massey
Alan Matthews
Bill Matthews
Jolie Matthews
Kim Matthews
Winnie & Gerald Matthews
Anna Matuszczyk
Dave Maud
Dean Maude
Jamie Mawer
Stephen Gary Mawer
Jonathan May
Peter May
Samantha May
Andrew Mayne

Debbie Mcbride
David McCallig
James McCann
James McCann
Lizzie McCormack
and Ashley Clegg
Courtney McCrickard
Mark McDermott
Paul McDermott
Stan McDermott
Daniel James McGuire
Simon McElroy
Duncan McFarlane
Callum McFaul
Jordan McGlynn
Keith McGrath
Kirsty McGrath
Ben McGuire
Steve MAC McGuire
David McHale
Mat Mchale
James McHugh
Mark McHugh
Robert McHugh
Ian McInnes
Ian McInroy
Scott McInroy
Peter McKay
David McLean
James McManus
Andrew McNichol
Peter McNichol
Jack McQuillan
Terry McQuillan
Clive McVay Robson
Giles, Harry & Robert Mcvicar
David Meades
Carl Meadows
Alex Meek
Conor Meese
Roz Megson
Paul Merritt
Dan Messenger
Callum Metcalf
Ashley Metcalfe
Bill Metcalfe
Bill and Jean Metcalfe
Luke Adan Metcalfe
Malcolm Metcalfe
Aimee Middleton
Robert Middleton
Paul Midwood
Tim Midwood
Claire Milburn
Mikey Millar
Terry Millett
Paul Milligan
Tony Milligan
Barry Mills
Kirsty Lee Mills
Chris Milner
Archie Milner
Emma Milner
David Rhino Milnes
Paul Milnes
Al Mitchell
Alan Mitchell
Amber Mitchell

Brian Mitchell
Laura Verity Mitchell
Wayne Thomas Mitchell
Richard Mizen
Robert Molineaux
Nikola Monaghan
Shane Monkman
Jo Monks
Dylan Mooney
Connor Rhinos Moore
Diane Moore
Doreen Moore
Joanne Moore
Phillip Moore
Neil Morgan
Les Morrell
Lisa Morris
Luke Mortimer
Stephen & Julie Morton
Michael Mosley
Laura Mackinnon Moss
Neal Moss
Beki Moulton
Carl Mountford
 Mudder
David Muhl
Sue Munden
Ross Munro
Simon Munro McCaskill
Janet Munro, Brian Munro
Jamie Munroe
Neil Murgatroyd
Alan Murphy
Carl Murphy
Emma Murphy
John Murphy
Lee Murphy
Margaret Murphy
Tracy Murphy
Alan Murray
Lisa Murray
Sarah Murray
Terence Myatt
Andy Myers
Christine & Ben Myers
Jake Myers
John Myers
Louise Myers
Paul M Myers
Peter Mylan
Ian Naughton
Lee Naughton
Claire Naylor
David Naylor
Scott Naylor
Tom Naylor
Les Neal
Alan Neesom
Simon Nelson
Aaron David Nesbitt
Joshua David Nesbitt
William Nesbitt
Gary Nevison
Graeme Nevison
Daniel Newband
Mark Newbound
Andrew James Newby
Graham Newby

William James Newby
Harry Newman
Tony Newman
Russell Newsome
Carol Newton
Margaret & Charlie Newton
David Nicholls
Antony Nicholson
Jonathan Nicholson
Martin Nicholson
Vicki Nield
Sheila Nielsen
Donna Niesyty
Juliusz Nitecki
Carl Noble
John Nolan
Mitchell Noon
Cat Norman
Andrew North
Chris North
Charlotte Norton
John M Nothers
Philippe Nourry
Paul Nugent
Emily Nutt
Georgina Nuttall
Finn O'Brien
Jordan O'Brien
James O'Donnell
Kevin O'Donnell
Justin O'Halloran
Robert O'Hara
Susan O'Hare
Ian O'Hare
Stephen O'Keefe
Kavan O'Reilly
Chris Oakes
Andrew Oakley
Dave Oakley
Anthony Oates
Debbie Oates
Donald S. Oates
Ann Ogden
Daniel Ogden
Keith Olbison
Blake Oldfield
Oldknow Family
Roger & Diane Oldroyd
Pierre Olesqui
Donna Elizabeth Oliver
Antoni Olkiewicz
John Olkiewicz
Josef Olkiewicz
John Ollerenshaw
Bruno Onteniente
Wilfred Orange
Emma Ormsby
Daniel Osborne
Jean Osborne
Dale Ossitt
Peter Overton
Samantha Overton
Becky Oxley
R Padgett
Simon Paget
Dean Painter
Tony Palin
Donna Marie Pallister

Steven Pallister
Darren Palmer
Des Palmer
Andrew Parker
Claire Parker
Joe Parker
Laura Parker
Louise Parker
Maf Parker
Melanie Parker
Michala Parker
Rita Parker
Terence Parker
Tom Parker
Alan Parkin
Stuart Parmenter
Kevin Parsons
Graham Pashley
Elliot Paterson
David Pattison
Leslie Paul
Megan Paul
Neil Paul
Gill Pawson
Andrew Payne
Diane Payne
Graham Payne
Bob Peace
Bev Pearce
Craig Lee Pearce
Philip Pearce
Alex Pearson
Darren Pearson
David Pearson
In memory of Geoff Pearson
James Pearson
Hazel Pearson
Myles Pearson
Steph Pearson
Trevor Pearson
William Pearson
Jonathan Peart
Michael Peat
David Pethullis
Andrew Petty
Andrew Phillips
Gail Phillips
Kevin Phillips
Kirsty Phillips
Keith Philpott
Gary Phipps
Julia Pickard
Tony Pickard
Alice Pickering
Claire Pickering
Anne Pickles
Ian Pickles
Beverley Pilbeam
Charlotte Pilbeam
Jamie Pill
Richard Pinder
Richard Pink
Chloe Pinkney
Eric Piper
George Pltts
Jonathan Pitts
Liam Pitts
David Pizzey

Angela Place
Miss Clare Playford
Miss Rebecca Playford
Trevor Playford
John L Plummer
Trevor Pollard
Brian Porter
Jack Pottage
Dianne Potter
Ian Potter
Philip Potter
Tom Potter
Matt Potts
Richard J Poulter
Chris Pounder
Tim Powell
Johnny Pratt
Allan Preston
Beki Price
Nathan and Andrew Pride
Alan Priestley
David Priestley
Andrew Prince
George Pringle
Steve Prior
Anne Procter
Danny Procter
Jem Procter
Leanne Procter
Steven Procter
Richard Proctor
Keith Pugmire
Mathew Pullan
Steven Pullan
Stu Pullan
Alexandra Pyett
Paul Pym
Kevin Quinell
Laura Quinn
Marina Lily Raddon
Anthony Rainford
Stephen Ralph
Michelle Ramsden
John Ramshaw
Ashley Randal
Natalie Randall
Jason Randles
James Ranns
Dawn Ratcliffe
James Rattenbury
Ben Rawcliffe
Darren Rawes
Ben Rawling
David Rawling
Chris Rawson
Marion Reape
Pat Redgate
Andrew Reece
David Reeder
Pete Reeder
Gwyn Rees
Adrian Reeve
Lee Reilly
Joy Render
Danny Reuben
Nigel Reucroft
Algie Reynolds
Andrew John Reynolds

Richard Reynolds
Christopher Rhodes
Samuel Rhodes
William Rhodes
Andrea Rich
Jonty Richards
Andrew Richardson
David Richardson
John Richardson
Kelly Richardson
Peter Micheal Richardson
Terence Richardson
Bernard Richmond
Emma Rigby
Catherine Riley
Dave Riley
Robert Riley
Will Riley
Michael Rimmington
Leslie Ripley
Kevin Rishworth
Claire Roberts
David Roberts
Irene Roberts
Janet & Trevor Roberts
Jos Roberts
John Roberts
Keith Roberts
Lee Roberts
Lynne & Keith Roberts
Mick Roberts
Nigel Roberts
Paul Roberts
Peter Roberts
Richard & Jen Roberts
Daniel Robertshaw
John Robertshaw
Malcolm Robertshaw
Philip Robertshaw
Claire Robertson
James Robertson
James Scott Robertson
Thomas Robertson
Ben Robins
Dean Robinson
Gemma Robinson
Janet Robinson
John Robinson
Joseph Robinson
Keith Robinson
Laura Robinson
Paul Robinson
Peter Robinson
Tony Robinson
Will Robinson
Nathan Robson
Chris Roby
Andrew Rock
Iain Rodgers
Mark Rodi
Evie Rogers
Brendon Rolfe-Betts
Andy Rollinson
Brian Rollinson
David Romans
Jennifer Roper
Jennifer Rose
Ian Ross

Jen Rossington
Steve Routledge
Kev. Rowberry
Steve Rowe
Robin Rowland
Ivor Rowlands
Joyce Rowlands
Chris Rowley
Richard Rowley
Andrew Rowney
Helen Rowney
Roger Rowsby
Matthew Royston
Amanda Rudd
George Rudd
Joshua Rudd-Watson
Nicola Ruddock
Rugby League Express
Michael Rush
Chris & Lynne Russell
Elizabeth Rutter
Eleanor Ryder
Paul Ryder
Dave Ryland
Darren Sables & Luther
Ellie May Sadler
Jack Sadler
Jonathan Saint
John Saker
David Salisbury
Neil Salvin
Liz Sanders
Gary Sanderson
Malcolm Sanderson
Sam and Darren Sanderson
Sonia Sanderson
Steven Sandiforth
Gemma Sarsfield
Adrian Saunders
Lee Saunders
Luke Saunders
Oscar Sawyer
Lee Saxton
Robert Scales
Dave Scanlon
Garry Scargill
Wayne Scargill
Henry L Schmid
Ash Schofield
Brian Scholefield
Paul Scholefield
Alan Scholey
Denise Scholey
Heather Scholey
Jon Schwind
Adrian Scott
Elaine Scott
Hannah Scott
Jean Scott
Matthew Scott
Michael & Brenda Scott
Mike Scott
Richard Scott
Robert Scott
Ronald Scott
Stuart Scott
Martin Scrimshaw
Phil Scurrah

Jacob Seaman
Phil Searle
P C Searle
Betty Seaton
Harold Sedgwick
Kathryn Seed
Chris Selby
Geoff Senior
Jonathan Senior
Steve Senior
Trevor Senior
Craig Lee Sewell
Mark Shackleton
Neil Shackleton
Shane Shann
Jane Sharkey
Mike Sharkey
Ann Sharp
Derek Sharp
Ian Sharp
Rob Sharp
Bill, Martyn and Richard Shaw
Dennis Shaw
Lesley Shaw
Mike Shaw
Nigel Shaw
Richard Shaw
Samantha Shaw
Susannah Shaw
Andrew Sheail
Barry Sheard
Karen Sheard
John B Sheffield
John Sheldon
Julie Sheldon
Michael Sheldon
John Shelmerdine
Julian Shepherd
Shelley Shiers
Craig and Archie Shippin
Jonathan Shires
Michael Short
Kevin Shyne
Ben Sibley
Maralyn Sidebottom
Richard Sidebottom
Seth Sikorski
Stuart Simmons
Nicholas Simonard
Tony Simons
Ali Simpson
Dan Simpson
Keith Simpson
Martin Sinfield
Rakesh Sinha
Terry Sizeland
Catie Skelly
Claire Skelly
Martin Skinns
Susan Skitt
Chris Slade
Fred Slade
Mark Slater
Nigel Slater
Robert Sloan
Gordon Smart
Alan Smith
Albert Smith

Albie Smith
Alicia Helen Smith
Andrew Smith
Ben Smith
Claire Smith
Craig Smith
David Smith
Dinah Smith
Hilary Smith
Ian Smith
James Smith
Janet Smith
Kate and Sophie Smith
Kevin Smith
Laura Smith
Louise Smith
Marc Smith
Mhairi Smith
Michael Smith
Olivia Smith
Paul Smith
Paul Matthew Smith
Peter Smith
Stephen Smith
Anthony Smithers
Kathryn Smithers
Deborah Ann Snowden
Clare Spacey
Richard Spedding
Benjamin Speight
Chris Speight
Debra Speight
Oliver Speight
Nick Spen
Bryan Spence
Paul Spence
Neil Spencer
Paul Spencer
Ruth Spinks
Donna, Chloe & Natasha Spinks
Chris Spivey
Colin Spofford
Sarah Spowage
Margaret Spray
David Springham
Janet Spurling
Anthony Stainsby
Mark Standley
Alice Stansfield
Mark Stansfield
Phil Stansfield
Amie Staples
Margaret Stapylton
Alan Stathers
James Stead
Lewis Stead
Martin Stead
Michael Stead
Francesca Stephan
Harriet Stephan
David Stephenson
Gary Stephenson
Mark Stephenson
Sarah Stephenson
Wayne Stephenson
Saul Stern
Mark Stevens
Nathan Stevens

Harvey Stevens
Richie Stevens
Tom Stevens
John Stevenson
Diane Stewart
Emma Stewart
John Stewart
Kay Stewart
Roy Stewart
Neil Stirk
Craig Stocken
Dale Stones
Gary Stones
Richard Storey
Wayne Storr
Alison Stott
Andrew Stott
Granville Stott
Jacob Stott
James Stott
Kath Stott
Nigel Stott
Jay Strain
Charlie Strange
Luke Strange
Marion Strange
Sally Stratton
Matthew Adam Straughan
David Stringer
Keith Stuart
John W Studd
John & Jane Sturdy
Leigh Sugden
Sarah Summers
Julie Summerscales
Mark Sunley
Mark Sutherland
Benjamin Swaby
Becky Swain
Janet Swales
Phil Swallow
Stephen Swalwell
John Richard Swann
Karen, Ellie and Alexandra Swann
Steven 'swinny' Swinburne
Robin Sykes
Paul Sykes, Heather Munro
Wendy Syson
Elizabeth Taft
Lindsay Tait
Debbie Tarbatt
Simon Tarbatt
Arnold Tate
David Tate
Jessica Tate
John Tate
Mark Tate
Suzanne Tate
Samuel Tatham
Liam Tattersall
Anthony Taylor
Catherine Taylor
Christine Taylor
Coen Taylor
Danny Taylor
David Taylor
E A Taylor

Heather Suzanne Taylor
Howard Taylor
Ian Taylor
Jeffrey Taylor
Kris Taylor
Lisa Taylor
Martin Taylor
Matthew Taylor
Michael Taylor
Nick Taylor
Phil Taylor
Richard Taylor
Sean Ross McCorrie Taylor
Danny Teasdale
Alan Tebbutt
Philip Tebbutt
John Teggart
Sarah-Jane Telfer
Stephen Telford
Jenny Temperton
Brian Tempest
Andrew Tennant
Craig Tennant
Kay Thackray
Sally Thackray
Philip Theobald
Kevin Thewlis
Dean Thomas
Julia Thomas
Adrian Thompson
Alan Thompson
Arthur Thompson
Ben Thompson
Beth Thompson
Brian Thompson
Chas Thompson
Francis Thomson
Karl Thompson
Kayleigh Thompson
Keith Thornhill
Mark Thompson
Martin Thompson
Paul Thompson
Philip Thompson
Sian Thompson
Steven Thompson
David Thornton
John Thornton
David Thorp
Graham Thurley
Malcolm Thurley
Jon Tinnion
Nicola Titley
Suzanne & Steve Tobin
David Todd
Mark Todd
Nick Todd
Peter Todd
Pep Tolmie
David Tomlinson
Shaun Tompkins
Chris Toothill
Jack and Edward Toronczak
Bob Torraca
Tony Torraca
Carole Towler
Glenn Town
Michelle Townsend

Ian Trainor
Chris Travis
Vicky Traynor
John Trevor
Leigh Treymaine
Malcolm Trigg
Mark Triggs
Lee Tromans
Kevin Trory
Keith Trow
Christine Tucker
Sarah Tucker
Sarah Tuke
Roy Tulloch
Gordon Turnbull
Daniel Turner
Glen Turner
Matt Turner
Steve Turner
David Twigg
Mick Underhill
John Underwood
Evelyn Utting
Margaret Varley
Michelle Varley
Chris Venner
Brian Verity
Gerald Vickers
Peter Vickers
Pete Vickers
Taginder Virdee
Andy Waddington
Steve Waddington
Dennis Waddle
Bev Wade
Mark Wade
Jack Wadsworth
Matthew Wadsworth
Nik Wadsworth
Sam Wadsworth
Samantha Wadsworth
Christopher Wain
Ben Wainwright
Paul Wainwright
Richard Wainwright
Adam Waite
Mark Waite
Michael Waite
Keith Waites
Lesley Wakefield
Thomas Walden
Joe Waldron
Sarah Waldron
Phil Wales
Alan J Walker
Alex Walker
Amelia Walker
Anthony Walker
Danny Walker
Debbie Walker
Ernie Walker
Granville Walker
James Walker
Jamie Walker
Julie Walker
Lisa Walker
Mark Walker
Michael Walker

Richard Walker
Sara Walker
Stephen Walker
Graham Walkington
David Waller
Steve & Bridget Waller
Martin Wallis
Peter Walls
Thomas Walsh
Simon Walter
Caroline Walters
Andy Walton
Becky Walton
Christine Walton
Colin Walton
John Walton
Kevin Walton
Malcolm Walton
Paul Walton
Tom Walton
Adam Ward
Bernard Ward
Charlotte L Ward
Ian J Ward (Thorner)
Jane Ward
Paul Ward
Andrew Wardle
Patrick M. Wardman
Peter Wardman
Emma Wareing
Chessie Warham
Zoe Waring
Bernard Warr
Dave Warren
Joel David Waterhouse
Mark Waterhouse
Emma Waterworth
Michelle Watkins
Andi Watson
David M Watson
Emma Watson
Matthew Watson
Maureen Watson
Michaela Christine Watson
Paul R Watson
Peter Watson
Trevor Watson
Jude Watts
Stu Watts
Harry, Jacob and Alex Waugh
Terry Webb
Harry Webster
Paul Webster
Sylvia Webster
Ian Weir
David Wells
Beverley Welsh
Danielle Welsh
Peter Welsh
Neil R. West
Rob Weston
Jamie Westwood
Ethan Wetherell
Richard Wetherell
Katie Wetherill
Tony Wharton
Adele Wheatley
Linda Wheatley

Robert Wheatley
Michelle Whipp
Kevin Whitaker
Peter Barry Whitaker
Simon Whitaker
Andy White
Anthony White
Martin White
Susan White
Donna Whitehead
Kevin Whitehead
Craig Whiteley
Michelle Whitfield
Andrew Whitham
Martin Whitham
Dr Martin Whitham
Stephen Whiting
Clive Whittaker
Leon Whyke
Rob Whytock
Ramsay Wieliczko
Stefanie Wigglesworth
Alex & Abbie Wightman
Betty Wightman
Allan Wilby
Ricky Wilby
Joe and Martin Wilcock
Jane Wilding
Ian Wilkey
Phil Wilkins
Alma Wilkinson
Alfie Wilkinson
Andrew Wilkinson
David Wilkinson
Graham Wilkinson
Jason Wilkinson
Liz Wilkinson
Mick Wilkinson
Nigel Wilkinson
Paul Wilkinson
Richard Wilko Wilkinson
Tim Wilkinson
Tom Wilkinson
Graham Wilks
Keith Wilks
Roy Wilks
Andy Williams
Dave Williams
Gary Kevin Williams
Gemma Williams
Lee Williams
Marc Williams
Martin Williams
Mervyn Williams
Chris Williamson
Doug Willis
Lisa Willis
Rachel Willsdon
Andrew Wilson
Anthony Wilson
Eddy Wilson
Freddie Wilson
Janet Wilson
Jean Wilson
Josh Wilson
Leo Wilson
Luke Wilson
Martyn Wilson

Mervyn Wilson
Michelle Wilson
Natalie Wilson
Nigel Wilson
Paul Wilson
Paul Richard Wilson
Peter Wilson
Steven Wilson
Steven Patrick Wilson
Thomas Wilson
Luke Winstanley
Simon Winter
Gemma Wittkowski
David Wolstenhulme
Denise Womersley
Andrew Wood
Danny Wood
Evie Wood
Jack Wood
Josh Wood
Stuart Wood
Tim Wood
Mitchell Woodham
Chris Woodhead
Winnie Woodhead
David Woodward
Woody
Andrew Wool
Steven Woolner
Graham Wordsworth
Neil Wormald
Harry Wormwell
Ben Marshall Worsnop
Scott Marshall Worsnop
Chib Worsnop
Debra Worthington
Kevin Wray
Paul Wren
Dean Wright
Ernest Wright
Lauren-Jane Wright
Lee Wright
Lewis Wright
Lisa Wright
Pam Wright
Stuart Wright
Jacob William Wroe IW, SW, GW
Chris Wroot
Debbie Wurr
Robert Wyard
Andrew Yardley
Gary Yates
Ellis Aaron Yeadon
Jennifer Yildizhan
Raising funds for Yorkshire Cance Centre
Dean Yorwerth
Dave Young
Helen Young
Matty Young
Stephen Young
Nicola Zajdler
Liam, Lukie, Jesse and Ryan